Building a Successful Career in Scientific Research

From Ph.D. student to post-doc, Phil Dee has been sharing his career
experiences with fellow scientists in his regular and highly acclaimed
Science's Next Wave column since 2000. Now his invaluable and
entertaining advice is available in this compact warts-and-all guide to
getting your science Ph.D. and subsequent post-doctoral employment as
a researcher. Phil Dee offers you the inside track on what life in the lab is
really like, with down-to-earth suggestions for making the most
productive use of your time, dealing with personal relationships in
science and maintaining your morale, as well as dealing with more
practical issues like how to design a really good poster for a conference.
As well as being based on the author's own experiences of working at
the lab bench, in front of the computer and the conference hall lectern,
the book brings together a wealth of advice from other young (and old)
scientists who have made it in science, and from a few who haven't. The
book has deliberately been written without reference to specific
scientific subjects and will therefore be accessible to all early career
scientists worldwide.

Phil Dee reinvented himself as a scientist after his previous jobs in the
world of finance failed to stimulate his career aspirations. He now holds
a first class honors degree in biology and a Ph.D. in molecular cell
biology, along with a growing collection of prizes, awards, and grants
bestowed on a successful young scientist. He started writing about his
career experiences in the world of science after a chance encounter with
a Next Wave editor unearthed Phil's extraordinary track record of
talking with all sorts of people in science and his gift for seeing
science as it is. Phil currently works as a post-doctoral research fellow in
the UK.

Building a Successful Career in Scientific Research

A Guide for Ph.D. Students and Post-docs

PHIL DEE

With cartoons by Chris McLeod

next wave *now part of:*

CAMBRIDGE UNIVERSITY PRESS
Cambridge, New York, Melbourne, Madrid, Cape Town, Singapore, São Paulo

Cambridge University Press
The Edinburgh Building, Cambridge CB2 2RU, UK

Published in the United States of America by Cambridge University Press, New York

www.cambridge.org
Information on this title: www.cambridge.org/9780521851916

First published 2006

Printed in the United Kingdom at the University Press, Cambridge

A catalogue record for this publication is available from the British Library

ISBN-13 978-0-521-85191-6 hardback
ISBN-10 0-521-85191-2 hardback
ISBN-13 978-0-521-61740-6 paperback
ISBN-10 0-521-61740-5 paperback

To Jo.
It's not about us.

Contents

Foreword

Being successful in science is an acquired trait. No one is born an eventually successful scientist. Some people may be better endowed than others with core traits that help lead to success: Being very smart is useful, and we know there's a genetic contribution to intelligence. Some people seem to be temperamentally more creative than others. But just being smart and creative does not ensure stardom in science. Just as one has to learn the substance of one's field and the details of scientific methods and technologies, there is much to learn about science as an enterprise and a community of diverse individuals.

There is a sequence of educational phases one must go through before becoming an independent researcher, and much to know about how to thrive at each stage. The scientific community has its own set of unique values and behavioral norms. These need to be learned and incorporated into one's way of working and dealing with one's colleagues. Speaking of one's colleagues, scientists can be an extremely competitive bunch of people, and there is much to be learned about working within that club.

Finally, being a scientist is not a unitary thing. Science provides a very wide variety of wonderful career options, although few people really are aware of the breadth of them. Scientific careers can also be quite complex and take many different forms. Few people only do research. Most do some combination of researching, teaching, giving talks, and serving on institutional and organizational committees, often at the national or international level. Working in a university is quite different from being a scientist in industry.

Scientific training is almost always only about the substance and methods of one's discipline. There are very few formal courses about the culture of and careers in science. Some mentors do a very good job helping their students prepare for life in the real world of research, but others seem to think one should learn on the job.

About a decade ago, the staff of AAAS and its journal, *Science,* recognized the need for a resource where scientists could turn for comprehensive career advice. They created the website called *Science*'s Next Wave. This site contains a very wide array of up-to-date articles written for developing scientists around the world interested in careers in academia, government and industry settings. Pairing *Science*'s Next Wave with its partner job-posting site, called *Science* Careers, enabled AAAS to offer the most comprehensive career resources available to scientists from the entire spectrum of fields.

One very popular feature of *Science*'s Next Wave has been the regular columns by Phil Dee. Collected together in this book, they provide a wonderfully written guide to navigating the pitfalls and paths to success in the very complex and competitive set of careers that make up the scientific enterprise. The style is light, the tone at times quite witty, but don't underestimate the wealth of information and frequency of useful insights. This is a book that should be read by every scientist, preferably before they get too far along in their developing careers.

Alan I. Leshner, Ph.D.
Chief Executive Officer, American Association
for the Advancement of Science
Executive Publisher, *Science*

Preface

I love being a scientist. It's the most infuriatingly rewarding profession on the face of the earth and daily drives me mad. Science is full of people like me, concentrating really hard on usually abstract subject matters. They are busy and often preoccupied. This makes maintaining relationships less than easy. Throw in the lack of a stable career path, lower than average financial rewards, often repetitive, boring work and more personal rivalry than you'd find in a large multi-national company and it can seem a daunting prospect for any newcomer. But the payback is great if you can hang in there. I don't care what anyone says, science is about the massive rush you get when you see something previously unseen by anyone; end of story. This book is intended to help the novice scientist wise up fast when they find themselves facing the seemingly impenetrable and incomprehensible world of science for the first time. It's also about cutting it as a professional scientist once you've jumped all the fences and 'been approved', however long that process is supposed to take in your particular institution and country. In between these two extremes lies a plethora of down-to-earth and sometimes humorous advice. I make no apologies for taking a sideways look at science – it often needs it.

This book emerged from a series of articles I wrote for the AAAS's *Science*'s Next Wave web magazine whilst studying for my Ph.D. and working in my first post-doctoral position. The advice and suggestions in this book are based on my own experiences as a developing scientist and on the countless informal 'interviews' I have conducted during my own private research into how science works. I would like to thank all the people, both humble and egotistical, who influenced my thinking during the long backbreaking years of study and research when I reinvented myself as a scientist. I now know who I am. Without their unwitting input I would not have such a clear idea of what on earth happened to me in these past few years. My sincere thanks to Kirstie Urquhart for that impromptu chat at the conference that led to the Next Wave column and for all she has done since. Thank you also to Elisabeth Pain, Anne Forde and Katrina Halliday.

To my wife and family I can only say, you know that I know what's really important. I love you all.

PART I

The first couple of years

Choosing and handling your Ph.D. adviser

Let's be upfront about one of science's biggest taboos: science can be unbelievably boring, especially other people's science. Doing most other people's Ph.D. or post-doc projects would simply drive many of us up the wall, so identifying your own is no trivial matter. Naturally, you become committed to your own projects partly because you know you just *have* to do the work. Hopefully, you are also genuinely interested in major aspects of your work; we all unconsciously ignore the boring bits to keep ourselves focused on the good stuff.

So an ideal start to a successful career at the 'coal-face' of human knowledge is to make sure that you pick a project that inspires you. Have you ever wondered why some people thrive on equations, whilst others are much happier staring down a microscope or trudging through the rainforest. What matters is that you identify your own little niche – somewhere you can work happily, animated by drive and passion for what you do. Finding the right project is a lot like falling in love: you might think you know what sort of person you'd go for, but that counts for nothing when your ultimate enchanter or enchantress walks in the room. Of my future partner my parents told me, 'You'll know when you know', and I have to say they were right.

Your journey of self-discovery begins when you set out to find a Ph.D. (No offence to final year undergraduates, but it's generally accepted that choice of first degree matters very little in the grand scheme of things.) I arranged a mini-tour of candidate universities when I was selecting my Ph.D. I looked at quite a lot

3

of projects and, not surprisingly, found most of them totally uninspiring. When I stumbled, downhearted, into my last port of call, I knew immediately that I'd found what I'd been looking for. The place, the person, and, most of all, the project all seemed 'right'.

If you are hunting for a Ph.D., cast your net far and wide, and be open-minded. You don't have to wait for adverts to appear. Get in first before the crowds. E-mail people or get on the telephone to arrange informal lab visits. If they're impressed with you, they might not even bother with the cost and hassle of advertising the position, and they'll love you for taking the initiative. Also, you may never have known they had a vacancy at all if you hadn't been proactive and picked a few promising names from the great panoply of scientists on the Internet.

It's a mistake to apply for a particular project in response to an advert without first visiting the lab and talking to the project leader and, if possible, the rest of the team. Most labs are very welcoming, given that so few applicants bother to do it, and I am sure you will find it very helpful. Otherwise, how on earth are you going to know whether the project will drive you insane after three months? And it's not just about the techniques you'll be using, you also need to size up the lab culture. I mean, just how full on and driven are the rest of the lab members, or how laid-back is the atmosphere? There are both types of lab, and more, and, depending on your personality, any one of them could drive you crazy. Above all, choose wisely.

The same, of course, goes for your Ph.D. adviser, although the lab culture is likely to reflect his or her style. A good working relationship with your new Ph.D. boss is essential as much of your initiation into the 'real' world of science comes to you directly through them. The potential for this relationship is staggering; think about it. In the course of your Ph.D. you could have several hundred long and in-depth conversations, by phone and e-mail as well as face-to-face. Together you'll enjoy moments of exhilaration and suffer bitter disappointment.

As in dating, there are 'rules' for getting the best from your scientific nearest and dearest. The first three rules lay the foundations for a successful relationship. Not surprisingly, it's all about communication.

Rule 1: the ground rule: communicate with your boss

Will your adviser maintain their interest in you even after your several years of possibly less than world-class research? The answer can definitely be yes, but only if you work at maintaining the relationship. One of the most common ways to fail your Ph.D. is to become isolated from you boss. I've seen this happen once and it's not at all nice. The person in question fell out with their adviser and managed to eventually lose all contact with them – not a smart move. So, if you wish to avoid ending up working in the local supermarket, maintain at least a reasonable relationship with your boss so you can submit your thesis. Keeping them on board for the long haul also keeps you tapped into their scientific 'street knowledge' and their network of contacts. These vastly improve your job-hunting prospects. Your boss offered you the Ph.D., so they must have rated you. Without becoming a lap dog, aim to work at keeping them pleased that they chose you.

Rule 2: keep your boss informed

As you increase in confidence, you'll naturally drift free from the burden of checking everything with your boss before you do it. But, beware of a potential slippery slope, especially if your boss is geographically distant from you. Sometimes you can go for days, weeks, or even months, without your boss knowing what you've been up to. What's more, even if you are a workaholic like me, the subconscious temptation is to let things slip when your boss is out of town. This nasty habit can lead to a false sense of independence ('I've got plenty of time and I'm in control') and a boss with a false sense of security ('I've not heard anything from them so I assume everything is OK'). Regularly feed information to your boss, if only by e-mail, to focus your mind on exactly how much, or how little, you have achieved since the last time you told them anything. Schedule this event once a week to give you a regular, and scary, target to aim for. There's no fear like the fear of admitting, 'I haven't achieved (or even worse 'done') anything at all since last week.' Applying this rule is a discipline that leads to happier students ('Regularly telling my boss what I've achieved seems to be really driving my project forward') and happier bosses ('I don't have to hope they are making progress, I know they are'). Establish this dialogue early in your relationship and you'll reap the benefits by pushing your project forwards faster.

Rule 3: discover what makes your boss tick

To get this new relationship working really efficiently, you'll need to find out which sort of scientific animal you are dealing with. Underneath a scientist's often quiet exterior lies constant mental activity. But is your boss an aggressive activist, who is always looking for their next experimental 'fix', or a more cautious completer-finisher, who only moves on to the next level when everything else is in place? Find out which of these, or the many other personality types, they are. By all means chat discretely with any 'old-hands' in the lab to assess their dealings with your boss, but the real meat of Rule 3 is subtle in the extreme – it's about your ability to communicate with the head honcho in their language. I learnt, to my cost, that I could utterly confuse my boss unless I chose my words very carefully. I'm still not clear how 'I don't think that experiment is worth repeating' sounds like 'I'll do it again straight away', but in time I learnt how to phrase things so they were crystal clear, a sort of 'boss-speak' I suppose. In effect, you'll need to identify where your personality and communication skills are at odds with your boss's and take steps to iron out the differences. As the student, the onus is on you to do this, not on them. Finally, do not make the mistake of underestimating your boss. After all, group leaders have made a successful career out of drilling for oil in nature's uncharted depths so give them a bit of respect and take time to scratch the surface.

Rules 4 through 6 propel you into a more dynamic student – boss relationship.

Rule 4: earn your boss's respect

Being lazy, unreliable or just plain obnoxious will not earn your boss's respect. But the most common problem for Ph.D. students is a lack of confidence. I once knew a capable student who used to kow-tow habitually to his boss's ideas simply because he lacked the conviction to believe in his own. This boss was equally frustrated by this student's lack of initiative. Earning your boss's respect doesn't only come from amassing lots of good results, important as they are; in science, it's all about showing you are capable of independent thought. So don't hamper your chances of career progression by either not believing in your ideas or lacking the bottle to speak up. Develop the knack of approaching your boss with good hypotheses and suggestions. Rule 4 is not about trying to 'sell' your boss every idea that comes into your head. They'll soon get tired of you. Why? Because we are all human and very few of us have really good ideas more than once a fortnight (see Chapter 16). So be prepared to hold your tongue and wait until you know deep down inside that you've got something good.

Rule 5: assert yourself

Many students are not used to making demands of people in positions of authority and can be far too submissive. If you apply Rule 4 you have the immediate advantage of being in a much stronger bargaining position: your boss respects you for your ideas. But remember that you are being trained to be an independent research scientist. So forget the old-fashioned student – teacher relationship, this is something new. When

7

appropriate criticise their rationale and argue your case. Stand your ground with your boss and you'll boost your confidence for when you have to stand your ground in front of a packed conference hall. Without being hardheaded for the sake of it, negotiate with your boss about your project aims, your workload, anything. If you are new to tackling bosses, don't be too pushy. Get yourself on an assertiveness training course. This will show you how to listen to your boss, then use what they say to approach them in a way that will increase the chance of a successful outcome: you'll get what you need. If you are assertive in the true sense of the word, your boss will feel that they got what they wanted too.

Rule 6, the golden rule: write for your boss

The golden rule is obvious. If you want an easy ride with your boss, you have to be proactive about writing, especially writing papers (see Chapter 6). They applied for the funding and brought you in primarily to increase their own personal tally of papers. That's what everyone is judged on in science. Ultimately, that's what your boss hopes for from your project. If your boss already respects you and is used to you behaving assertively, early delivery of good-quality writing will utterly convince them that you are worth investing even more of their time in. So, as soon as your results are in, start collating them all together electronically.

Daunting as it may seem at first, you can write the draft outline of a paper within a week, if you put your mind to it. When I handed my boss the best part of my first paper, he was like a dog with two tails: I had a great working relationship with my Ph.D. boss, but I had never experienced this level of interest in my work before. Clearly nothing gets a scientist's attention like the prospect of submitting another paper with their name on it.

The golden rule (Rule 6) is the hardest to apply, but has the most wonderful effects. First, your boss will love you and gladly read several drafts of your thesis. Second, writing and defending your thesis will be a whole lot easier with at least some of your work submitted for publication (see Chapter 6).

So there's your complete six-step guide to becoming a good 'boss-handler'. Follow these rules and you'll be more likely to find yourself with a boss who is also your greatest ally.

2

Motivation, time management, and multitasking

Assuming you don't already know, sit down and work out your own personal reasons for putting yourself through a Ph.D. Once you discover what your true motives are, however trivial, never forget them. It may be a simple desire to see the title 'Dr' on a letter addressed to you. No matter. When you are up against it, it's that motive which will keep you going.

But, how do you translate this personal goal into a successful project? Scan a few job ads and you'll notice that the require-ment 'self-starter' pops up with surprising regularity. To have any hope of completing your Ph.D. within your allotted number of years, you need to have this quality in abundance. First, you need the self-discipline to plan your days, weeks, and months yourself. Second, you have to motivate yourself to stick to your plan for the long haul.

Here are a few strategies that help to maintain momentum.

The daily grind

Most Ph.D. projects begin with an easy experiment that stands a good chance of working. This is a good model for the working day: start each day with a simple task. Doing something straight-forward first thing gives your brain time to come online and builds your confidence if you can't face diving straight into a tricky experiment. However, once you've 'woken up' don't delay getting stuck-in; displacement activities can easily sneak in and fill up your entire day. You may convince yourself that you need to scan the recent journals in the library or tidy your bench, but,

10

if you have writing or experiments that need facing up to, then face up to them you must.

It helps if you can build some mental breathing space into your day. Time spent reflecting on your work is just as important as time spent actually working. A 15-minute walk can do wonders for your brain's oxygen levels, and it's often when real inspiration comes.

Try to finish each day with a positive outlook. If you're lucky, your day will end with a good result or a fresh new idea. This gives you an immediate boost the following morning. But, the end of the day is perhaps the worst time to push your luck. The law of averages is set against too many experiments working perfectly first time.

Your worst enemy is fatigue. It lowers your efficiency and makes you more prone to errors, and that's when self-doubt creeps in. So, when you're getting too tired, for goodness sake go home. And, if you can, try to make your home a place of respite from work. If you wake up in the morning to see a pile of unread papers bearing down on you from the bedside table, you'll soon feel that you've had a skinful of your Ph.D.

Of course, if you find yourself truly on a roll, you may wish to shelve the normal habit of quitting while you're ahead. After all, you never know how long the results will continue to flow in. It's certainly a rare treat to watch everything you touch turn to gold! Unfortunately, you can't plan for these work fests; they just happen when you least expect them! If late in the day your work does start to go wrong, change over to something that stands a better chance of letting you end on a high. Even if you only manage to plan or prepare for the next day's experiments, you'll get the sense of achievement you need. The golden rule is do something, anything, as long as it contributes to both your project and your sense of positivity. Always spend a few minutes at the end of the day plotting out the next day's work. Write it down.

If your daily work plan starts to feel a little stale, it sometimes pays to simply vary your routine. Try the odd late shift in the lab, or start ridiculously early now and again. This way you either earn yourself a lie-in or an afternoon off. Radical hours have a funny way of making you feel good about yourself, even though you're not clocking up any more total working time. Also, you'll be surprised how much you get done without other people around to distract you.

The long view

Contestants in endurance events need regular milestones to aim for, and there aren't too many of these in a Ph.D., so you need to set them for yourself, even if you are lucky enough to have an advisor who checks up on you regularly. It doesn't matter if your deadlines are self-imposed or artificial, as long as you set ones that motivate you. Simply aiming to complete a task by Friday really helps you look forward to your favourite weekend treat. And, by then you'll deserve it for knuckling down to work.

Early on in your Ph.D. comes the frustrating realisation that your science, any science, can move forward only in baby steps. Research rarely happens any other way, so learn to live with this fact. This actually helps with goal setting, as you can tackle your workload only in a long series of bite-sized chunks. An experienced scientist once told me to expect 80% of my best results in the final year of the project. She was right.

How do you keep on track when disaster strikes? Basically, learn to expect hold-ups and problems around every new corner. In fact, looking back, you'll be able to count the new techniques that worked first time on the fingers of one hand. But don't panic when things go horribly wrong – your failed experiments really are the springboard to success. Learning to get over such apparent disaster is a key part of your scientific training. Your best line of defence against utter dejection is simply to talk to people. After one disastrous morning in the lab, I was contemplating abandoning ship for the day when a random chat with someone in the corridor transformed me into a person crazed with the desire to get my experiment to work. Whatever you do, talk to someone.

To get a good Ph.D., you have to want it bad, real bad. But most important, remember the basics: eat, sleep, exercise, and relax. Keep yourself fresh to keep on course, and prove to would-be employers that you are that elusive creature: the self-starter!

Stepping up a gear

OK, so you might be thinking, what's the rush? You have at least three years to complete your Ph.D. But, be warned – you can't cram for this degree in the final year! I've watched a fellow UK Ph.D. student frantically trying to finish writing-up in the last few days of his fourth year. It's not that this person didn't put in the hours. He clearly had an active time and kept himself very busy. But a high level of activity does not necessarily equate to a high number of useful results. Had he been taught how to conduct highly efficient research and how to work more effectivly from the outset, he may already have had his photo taken in a floppy graduation hat. The ideal is to dream up the 'clincher': the feasible experiment with the most meaningful and informative output. But, even if the 'clincher' eludes you, there is still a lot you can do to increase your productivity.

You may feel frustrated at your own inability to work competently, or you may doubt that you can ever complete your thesis on time. If so, ask an experienced post-doc in your lab how they manage to do five different things in parallel without getting ruffled.

Of course, there's no quick fix to successful multitasking: the best way to become truly efficient at anything is practising it day-in, day-out for months. But understand and implement a few simple principles and you will come to experience the quiet 'rush' you get from knowing you are 'spinning plates' in the lab.

Not surprisingly, the first step to successful multitasking is getting really organised. If you don't know exactly where to find

13

your own stuff, you'll waste no end of time tracking down a particular reagent, experimental protocol or previous set of results. However you choose to organise your things, make sure you can locate almost anything you want at the drop of a hat. You must find what you need quickly and get back to adding value to your thesis with the minimum loss of momentum. The watchwords for your filing and storage systems are 'labelled' and 'accessible'.

We all need stocks and supplies, be it laboratory consumables or CD-ROMs to hold all your files. Make sure you have plenty of everything you need. Getting plenty means you avoid wasting time constantly replenishing your stocks. When planning an experiment, make a definitive list of all the stuff you need and then track down where you can get hold of it. This may take longer than the experiment itself, but efficiency wizards know the central importance of advance preparation, and they find what they need well in advance. This avoids unnecessary delays caused by a single missing component on the day of the experiment.

But, beware of wasting time, money, and effort trying to cover every possible eventuality. A good multitasker waits until the first possible moment the decision to do an experiment can be made with certainty, and only then starts to prepare for it. In the meantime, of course, they are doing a whole host of other things that they know will certainly, or almost certainly, need to be done. Constantly reappraise whether each intended activity is worth doing, or should be shelved. To do this you'll need to keep focused on your project goals in the face of seemingly endless possible activities.

It's easy to get sidetracked – I wasted several months of my Ph. D. trying to prove a point. My own doggedness caused me to pursue one experimental approach almost to the exclusion of everything else. I was saved from this dark, lonely tunnel by an offer of help from an overseas lab. They had solved my problem by adopting a different approach – one I had already dismissed

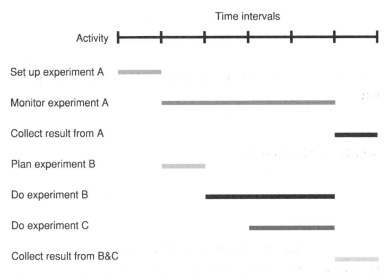

Fig. 1. Example of a Gantt chart. Horizontal bars represent both the timing and the duration of each task, enabling potential gaps, overlaps and conflicts to be easily identified in advance.

as too difficult. My advice is to prepare yourself mentally to drop months of work if you discover a better way to achieve your aims. And, to discover a better way, you'll have to keep an open mind, not to mention eyes, and ears (see Chapter 3 and Chapter 7).

By careful written planning, you can pack a lot more into a day than you can possibly achieve by thinking on your feet. Plan the next day's activities at the end of each day while it is still fresh in your mind. You'll avoid having to get out of bed in the early hours to note things down that you might otherwise forget! You may feel your lab note book is sufficient for your needs, but keep a diary to remind you what's happening next. Gantt charts (see Figure 1) are an excellent way to visualise how much work you can fit in. They work best for longer-term planning over weeks or months.

OK, so much for getting organized, but what about the sharp end of multitasking? When the pressure's really on in the lab, you'll need to rely on two things:

1 **A multifunction alarm timer**. Get a wristwatch with a timer function or timer that is permanently clipped on to your lab coat – you'll forget to take a normal stop-clock with you when you set off down the corridor and annoy everyone when it goes off in your absence. Countdown alarms work better than stop-watches, as they don't need you to remember to look at them. Set an alarm for a few minutes before each activity is due to end. As a check on this discipline, you can try to remain mentally aware of all your various tasks, but simply ticking items off your task list in the order you decided to do them is the best way to keep on track.

2 **Your lab note book**. Some people love to make meticulous neat notes in their lab books. I, and many others I have met, do not. Nevertheless, if you cannot find out (a) what you did last week and (b) how you did it, you are well and truly stuffed in this science game. So write down what you do, even if it's a bit scribbled. If you can answer the question, 'Do I know exactly what I did?', then stop fretting. Use a lab book with page numbers as this helps to track things down later.

When learning to multitask, don't try to tackle too much too soon. To begin with, it's much better to do one thing at a time, and do it really well. You can practise multitasking on things that don't really matter if they overrun (lest you forget about them). When you are more confident, try pushing your luck by running two experiments in parallel, then three, and so on. Remember, safety comes first, so only attempt what is safe and build in enough slack time to do each experiment slowly enough to do it well. If you have to rush it, you're taking on too much and it will probably end in disaster.

And, finally, when you get a good result, ensure that your experimental output is up to publication quality. If you don't, you'll only have to repeat the experiment later when you have more important things to worry about – like writing the manuscript (see Chapter 6).

Handling the literature

Ruthless reading

Even for hard-working scientists, projects usually move forwards quite slowly. However, there are an awful lot of scientists today. This means that keeping up to date with the output from this army of academics is a major challenge. As a Ph.D. candidate you are aiming to become nothing less than a world expert in your own research. You need to know your stuff. Any large pile of photocopied research papers is inherently unstable and liable to rearrange itself into a random order at the slightest provocation. Once you amass such a stack of unread papers, you will probably never get to the bottom of it. To get through a Ph.D.'s worth of reading, you need to develop surgical ruthlessness. Become relentlessly efficient with your reading and the sheer vastness of the ever-expanding literature can begin to seem manageable.

The first step in ruthless reading is to be disciplined about organising your regular hunting forays into the literature. Leave it too long between your paper harvesting sessions and you will reap too many to read in one week – then they begin to pile up. Citation and journal databases like the Web of Science (wos. mimas.ac.uk), and referencing software like Endnote (endnote. com) make literature searches and reference-handling a piece of cake. But, however good your software, you still need to know exactly what you are searching for. Compile a definitive list of your keywords and try including important authors' names as well as key scientific terms. Then, it's just a matter of remembering to run your complex search strings to pull out all the new articles. These periodic blitzes are a good way to keep up to date with the mass of the literature. As a complementary method to just blitzing the database, most journals offer free e-mail alerts every week or month to keep you informed about new papers. This is well worth doing for the major journals where most of your community publish, but subscribe to too many minor journals and your inbox will soon be bombarded with endless pages of contents that you'll probably never bother to look at.

Maybe it's the nagging doubt that your search strings are too restrictive, but don't ignore the occasional compulsion to enter the library and just let your instincts guide you. It's amazing how often I've stumbled on something directly relevant, apparently by good fortune. You may scoff, but it works!

Another great way to get yourself quickly in the picture when facing a new field is to start your search in the references section of your top ten favourite papers. The same principle applies to using recent review articles. Following relevant citations can lead to one almighty paper chase, but you can turn up some really spot-on stuff in this way. If you can find a lab that maintains an up-to-date list of references for your subject on its Web page (i.e., not just publications from that lab), so much the better.

The second step in ruthless reading is, well, getting around to reading it all. If you are anything like me, you download and print out papers first and ask questions later. If you do, don't amass one of those vast, not to mention slippery, piles of paper on your desk. You'll soon have no clue as to what gems and mysteries lie within the pile, as yet unread. Pluck up the courage to start sifting through it before you freak out at how long it will take you to read the stuff that catches your eye just in the first two inches of the stack. If you have one of these piles, it must be counted as one of the worst possible Ph.D. monsters: slay it before the mere thought of it haunts you.

Tackling your monster pile is straightforward, if difficult. Catch yourself in a decisive mood and dive in, sorting into piles labelled 'Essential', 'Nice to read if I get time', and 'Why did I even print this?'. It can help to put the papers in some sort of order, so you can easily find the one you need. Alternatively, keep the PDFs backed-up and sorted on you computer. You won't need to keep printing the same paper if you can't find the original, as subsequent rereads can often be done on-screen.

Even your ruthlessly reduced reading list may be quite a stack. If you are a slow reader, try increasing your reading speed (ucc. vt.edu/stdysk/suggest.html). In a nutshell, practice visually 'photographing' half a line, or even a whole line of text in one glance, and keep moving. Avoid rereading the same phrase or passage – you may do this more often than you realise. As your reading speed increases, you'll almost certainly increase your level of comprehension. This is because whole sentences make more sense to your brain than a string of individual words. With practice, you'll find yourself hunting the text for keywords or phrases that ring your mental alarm to slow down and read more carefully. In all but the most earth-shattering papers (for this sort I still have to sit down and read slowly) you'll probably be looking for no more than half a dozen pieces of information. If you are pushed for time, read the first and last sentences of each paragraph until you track down the section most relevant to your needs. This is where authors often stick the best stuff.

Find your own best time and place to read. Naturally, forget it if you're too tired or it won't sink in. The best policy is to read the important new papers quick and hard, quite literally as soon as you get hold of them. Then at least you've got a grasp on it for a later in-depth read. This rapid reading also makes you look on the ball; avoiding the embarrassment we all suffer when someone influential starts on about a hot new paper they assume everyone else has read. A little reading can go a long, long way. But, what about the other, less obvious, literature? What about the background reading? For less-pressing stuff, I often read

19

through a paper in the office or lab (whichever is quieter) during a short break, say 20 minutes, between experiments. You'll be amazed how many accumulated papers can trickle into your memory in the space of a few weeks.

Breaking the code of scientific writing

Scientific writing sends subtle but powerful signals to its more clued-up readership. The crux of this style is the use of understatement and cliché. You need to learn to recognise the hidden code in an otherwise straightforward-looking piece of writing. It was only once I started writing papers myself that I realised there are some real gem-like phrases out there. Here is a sample of classic scientific understatements and clichés:

'**A model system for studying**' Usually bandied around in introductions to talk up the system used in the investigation. The real question is whether the *system* is in fact a good *model*, and the answer may be rather subjective. Still, we all have to sell our work nowadays, so some authors might as well express their heartfelt opinion and claim that their system is a model or, if they are really pushy, a paradigm.

'**Important**' as in 'important new evidence'. All scientists like to think their work is important, but remember that, second only to international diplomats, scientists are the champions of understatement, so this word can be very evocative.

'**Necessary and sufficient**' This is a classic bombshell phrase used to describe in glorious simplicity a truly amazing result. It translates as, 'the result depends on this and nothing else'. I can only aspire to include this phrase in one of my papers some day!

'**Puzzling**' **or** '**intriguing**' These are positive words for describing inconsistencies or inexplicable results. 'Puzzling' suggests the authors have hit on an interesting anomaly. It may be worth giving this some further thought and testing any ideas you might have. 'Intriguing' is stronger and suggests the anomaly has 'got under the authors' skin', so to speak, and that they themselves may be more likely to follow it up with further experimentation.

'**Surprising**' Nature is often surprising, so why should we be surprised when scientists use the word 'surprising'? I guess it might be used to add a bit of kudos to the authors, on the assumption that the readers are convinced of their intellectual abilities. We might respond, 'If these guys find this result surprising, I'd better take note.'

'**Exciting**' Now just you steady on! Scientists aren't expected to get excited. Well, that's the stereotype. *Au contraire*, I say. In my experience, scientists often get very excited. This subjective word is often used to generate interest and enthusiasm in an area of research, rather than a specific result.

'**Our preliminary results suggest** . . .' Basically, the authors are admitting they have no strong evidence to back up this particular idea. Watch out though, this might be a hint that they have an ace up their sleeve, yet to be made public. In any case, this type of phrase can be a useful signal for competitors, telling them it might be worth trying to repeat what these authors did to see if the result is reproducible.

'**Taken together, these results show** . . .' This means: 'Stay with us here, we're trying to convince you there's a connection.' This phrase is handy when you want to try and bolster an argument by linking two supporting pieces of evidence pointing at the same conclusion.

'**It is tempting to speculate** . . .' This is a standard cliché that can be used in discussions as a get-out clause in case the ideas that follow are subsequently shown to be wrong. But, let's be crystal clear here. It is also often used to disguise lines of investigation that scientists may, even as we speak, be actively pursuing in that lab. If this really does describe wild speculation, why would anyone bother to say it in a scientific paper? You need to have at least a strong hunch about something before sticking your neck out like this.

Of course, these are just a few examples. The point is that you can, and should, find many more examples by reading the literature yourself. If you read things at face value and don't wise up to the hidden meanings in paper-speak, you might miss an opportunity to extend your own research. Worse, you might even get left behind if your field is one that moves on rapidly. Use every opportunity to consult experienced and trusted colleagues on what they think the authors mean when they use a particular word or phrase. This way you'll also learn another great lesson: different people interpret the same passage in different ways. So much for scientific papers being unambiguous and crystal clear!

4

Report writing

If you have to write a progress report at a relatively early stage in your research, for example during the first year of a UK Ph.D., you may believe that you haven't got much to say. How wrong you are! You have plenty to write about, even if your results are a little thin on the ground. The first year of your Ph.D. isn't about amassing results; it's about making all your mistakes in one big batch before you start your research proper. Unless, that is, you made all your mistakes during your M.Sc. and extensive pre-Ph.D. industrial experience!

But, ignoring your many weeks fouling-up in the lab, what have you got to show for your first year? Are you still not sure? Well, neither was I until I started writing my first-year report. This humble report was possibly the turning point in my Ph.D. What's more it made me realise just how much I enjoy writing. You may be asked to produce a brief or extensive report, written in either thesis-speak or in the style and format of a scientific paper. Whatever the challenge, this is probably the first time you'll need to get your act together and think about what you've done so far and why you've done it.

It's a good idea to start writing your materials and methods section first. This is unlikely to amount to much yet, but this stuff is relatively easy to get down on paper. It's also extremely useful if anyone asks you for your protocol. Remember, this section should only say *how* you did what you did and nothing about *why* you did it that way.

Starting to write your introduction may be one of the most difficult aspects of your Ph.D. This is where you set the scene by justifying why your problem is worth devoting three or more years of your life (and a whole lot of other peoples' money) to solving. Try to paint a picture of your project as addressing a gaping hole in the literature.

Faced with a plethora of relevant papers going back into the depths of time (or the last ten years, at least), where do you begin? Start by making a shortlist of key papers that you must mention due to their sheer importance. Build your introduction around these key papers. Beware of ending up with a list of references so extensive that nobody will believe you have read all of them! You only need to give one or two key references to make a point – stick to the most recent papers from the journals with the highest impact factor. Consider ending the introduction with a succinct hypothesis and a nice series of tests for it, e.g. does doing X show that Y occurs?

'Results!' I can still hear you screaming, 'But I haven't got any yet!' This early you've got some licence to elaborate on (but not exaggerate) what you have achieved. If necessary, you can 'puff up' what you have got by including a little extra detail. For example, you could include preliminary results from your latest experiments or devise an extra table or figure to make it easier for the reader to interpret what results you do have. Try to 'lump' your results together under sub-headings that could form the chapters in your thesis. This will be quite a difficult exercise so early in your Ph.D., and your output will probably bear no resemblance to your finished thesis, but it will certainly set you thinking. Remember to just describe each result and go on to the next one. There should be no discussion here. The word 'To' is a good linker to enable your writing to flow from one paragraph to another, e.g. 'To show that X happens, Y was done'. Don't write 'In order to', the word 'To' is fine just on its own.

Your discussion is where you remind the reader, in a nutshell, what you did and then say what it means. Discussions can be problematic to write early in your Ph.D., as they can become dumping grounds for all your ideas for future work. If you don't have a clue which of many different experimental approaches to follow, it will be painfully obvious here if you simply list them all. Try to think hard about what you can realistically achieve within the time you are allowed. Soon enough, it will be time to start winding down your research and write full time (if you want to submit in a timely manner). It's better to write more extensively about the most obvious experimental approach to take, and mention the other more risky options briefly. Your examiners will be thrilled to suggest that one of your alternatives might be better, but at least you've covered yourself by mentioning it. The knack is to spot the holes in your research – there are probably plenty at this stage – as these are where the examiners are likely to direct their questions at your final thesis defence. Don't forget to write a nice punchy concluding paragraph to hammer home the point of your report. Finish by writing your abstract (see Chapter 6), the shortest but most important part of this work.

Use your first-year report as a springboard for your thesis or first paper. You'll probably be faced with writing both of these sooner than you think, so get yourself up to base camp before you have to scale the inevitable writing mountain.

5

Powerful presentations

Successful oral presentations are not just about meticulous slide preparation, important as that is, they're also about doing a good 'head-job' on yourself. You don't want to wake up in a cold sweat the night before your talk.

Remember when you took your driving test or sat your final examinations? Sure, you needed to be alert and motivated; but, if your mental pendulum happened to swing too far in that direction, you may have ended up too 'charged-up' to be effective. You may have missed things and made mistakes in your eagerness to impress. Similarly, if you practised your deep-breathing exercises a little excessively, you may have faced the challenge with an attitude of 'it doesn't really matter, anyway'. I suspect most of us end up in the unhappy no-man's-land between these two extremes. We enter the arena neither motivated nor relaxed: we just get in a bit of a flap. The real trick is to find both states of mind within you and use them simultaneously. I know, I know, this is an unusual concept for us 'fight or flight' creatures – to stand our ground *and* keep our cool, but with some careful preparation it can easily be achieved, at least for a short time. Long enough to present an award-winning talk at any rate.

Here's a six-point checklist to make your presentation an enjoyable experience for both you and your audience!

1 **Identify your message**. Before you do anything, consider what, in a nutshell, you have discovered. Choose what to include,

26

and what not to include, very carefully. If you're honest with yourself and you've listened to your critics, you'll know which of your results are weaker and may leave you open to attack. You may not have time in your talk to explain yourself fully, so, even if the experiment was your 'baby', be bold enough to skip over it, or even leave it out altogether. If there's a particular aspect of your work that you'd like to receive feedback on, give it a more prominent place. Having now seen what you look like, people will approach *you* afterwards for a chat.

2 **Know your stuff.** Just by standing there you will be taken to be an expert in your field, so expect to be asked questions outside of your own work. You may wish you could bluff your way through the talk, but, take it from me, your lack of reading will be glaringly obvious when you are in the searchlight of an incisive question from the audience. The answer: read it now and don't regret it later. If you really don't have time to read *all* the papers, scan the abstracts and get the message and the keywords. Name-dropping a keyword may save your bacon on the day.

3 **Plan an elegant presentation**. The old adage is true: first tell the audience what you are going to talk about. Then talk about it. Then tell them what you said. To ensure your message gets through, it's essential to make your talk visually interesting. Once their eyes start dropping, your message has to rely solely on their ears, and ears aren't hot-wired into the brain like eyes. So don't expect them to look for too long at one slide, don't ask them to read too much text, and avoid the pace of your talk being too slow or too fast. A tried and tested format is to describe your research as a more-or-less chronological story. Adding small amounts of human interest increases attention span, and helps the audience warm to you.

4 **Make it look professional**, following the same simple rules as for poster design (see Chapter 7). Like it or not, science, as are many professions, is chock-full of people who won't even pay attention to you unless what you are showing them is bang up-to-scratch. Produce your presentation in Microsoft

PowerPoint® (office.microsoft.com). It's the easy-to-use industry standard and PowerPoint® projectors are everywhere nowadays. PowerPoint® also obviates the need to 'faff' around
mounting fiddly slides that always seem to end up upside-
down anyway. As an extra back up to your multiple CDs or
disks (don't rely on one), you can make colour overhead trans-
parencies of your PowerPoint® slides. Even keynote speakers
sometimes flounder when their PowerPoint® files won't open.

5 **Practise your delivery**. Be bold and speak up a bit. To get your
timings right, have several dry runs. This is easy with Power-
Point's® 'Rehearse Timings' function. Don't write down exactly
what you'll say – you'll only end up reading it and that'll make
everyone cringe. If the content of your slides isn't enough to
prompt you, simply print out your own annotated version of
each slide with keywords highlighted and any extra information you want to say. This way, you won't need to keep finding
the right place in your notes – it's right there in front of you in
exactly the same format as the presentation the audience is
seeing. As you won't spend more than a few seconds finding
your place, you'll look as if you're talking off the cuff, with one
or two quick glances at your notes. All very professional.

6 **Get your head straight**. OK, now you're well prepared, all you
have to do is give your talk. So what about this head-job? First
remember that, if you've been given a slot for a short talk,
you're only going to be up there for 20 minutes or so. Consciously deciding to let your nerves jangle just before you get
on your feet to speak might help you to avoid worrying beforehand. The plan is that by the time you stand up to talk, you'll
have too much to think about to worry for long anyway.
Sounds, unlikely? Try it; it's a mental trick that works. Remember to try to be alert and relaxed at the same time. Practise this
state of mind well before your talk to become familiar with the
feeling. Just say the words to yourself: I'm 'alert' but 'relaxed'.
Warning: it's so useful for interviews (see Chapter 17) and the
like that it can become addictive!

PART II

The end of the beginning

6

Writing papers and abstracts

We scientists can be slow in getting around to writing. We are totally absorbed in the search; it's what keeps us going. Most of us thrive on pushing back the perimeter fence of our own little field of research, even if our total estate only grows by a few square centimetres each working week. But this imaginary field is just that, imaginary; that is, unless we publish what we've discovered promptly. If we don't, we might find that we 'own' rather less of our field than we thought. Aside from hindering the progress of other scientists who could have built on our work, we might stuff up our career prospects by getting scooped. What's more, we might diminish the research standing of our host institution.

Playing a waiting game is all very proper when we need to check our results or are trying to save them up for a high-impact publication – but what if deep down it also has something to do with not liking the idea of knuckling down to writing? What if, secretly, we find it easier to keep on working in the lab than ever putting finger to keyboard? If we don't get down to writing, we are forgetting the true purpose of our job. We all listen with bated breath to explosive new data presented at a conference with a stack of supporting slides and a lot of panache; but, unless the paper eventually comes out, who will ever believe it? 'Ah, they must have been unable to confirm those results', we say.

31

Making rapid writing-up possible

To help you write up promptly follow these guidelines:

1 **Focus on success.** Being a winner is not just about following up the experiments that work the first time. These might not be that exciting. Develop the discernment to pursue those questions that, although they may be harder to crack, are crucial to getting a big paper out. The key is to face up to cutting down your hit list of outstanding experiments. WARNING: if you apply this principle, you must accept that you will NEVER be able to do some of the most interesting experiments that came to you in the middle of the night. Why? Because they are not that important (for 'important' read 'impact factor').

2 **Prepare your figures.** Each time you get a publishable result (definition of 'publishable': a reproducible result that arouses some excitement in your boss and that you know is 'real' because you've already proved it to yourself), prepare a figure or table and a brief legend *immediately* – or you most probably won't get around to it for ages, if ever. You'll not only make the most of that spare half an hour here and there fiddling with Excel® or Photoshop® but you'll also avoid the terrifying thought of preparing all your figures and tables from scratch. Beware another pitfall: if you have many similar results to choose from, you might kid yourself that you'll have time to go back and select the ideal representative for your figure. You probably won't. So, select 'the one' now and believe in it.

3 **Get up to speed with the literature.** Use other spare half hours to get together most of the literature you'll need to refer to in your introduction. If you're lucky, there'll be a big recent paper in your field that'll cite almost everything already and save you a lot of searching – make sure you don't miss it (see Chapter 3), but be sure to read anything you do end up citing.

4 **Remind yourself of your purpose.** Constantly remind yourself that the reason you get up in the morning is to write scientific papers. Even if you are not convinced that this is your end

game, remind yourself anyway. As for most forms of mental programming, it sort of rubs off.

5 **Get out of the lab**. Once you half-believe Point 4 you'll have to get over the next hurdle: convincing yourself that you are in a non-urgent situation in the lab. Lab work can get pretty frantic when things go wrong as well as when you're on a roll. The next experiment is always just begging to be done. But, even if you work in a very competitive field, things rarely move *that* fast. Finding time to write requires the same foresight as taking a well-earned holiday – your career won't stop just because you have. In fact, just like taking a much-needed rest at the right time, getting that paper out is likely to give your confidence and your research a massive boost.

6 **Set a deadline**. Remember, there's a law of diminishing returns with experimental results that clearly states another six months' work on the same thing will still not get you into *Nature* or *Science*. Let it go and accept what you've got. 'A bird in the hand . . .' as they say. Select and stick to a very tight deadline for submitting the paper. This way, you leave yourself with no choice but to drop everything else and plough on. It also forces you to identify those nasty little gaps in your results and focus on filling them in a bit sharpish – keeping you away from the ever-present temptation to wander down unrelated experimental paths.

Creating your paper

The carefully crafted sentence is a powerful communication tool. Yet, as a first-time author of primary scientific literature, you might be forgiven for thinking that writing a paper must be easy compared with compiling a thesis (see Chapter 8). Surely, scribing a few brief pages must be easier than amassing hundreds. But, what papers lack in quantity, they make up for in quality. A good paper can take very much longer to write than an equivalent piece of thesis. What's more, once written, it can take a long time to reach the printed page.

Long before you ever start writing a paper, you need to work out what it's going to contain. What's the main message you want your paper to get across, and which of your results support it best? List your selected results in case, to your horror, you find that you don't yet have them all in, or that the quality of your data, images, or statistical analyses is not up to scratch. Then review the boundaries of your paper, but don't spend too long pondering over what to include and what to leave out. Whatever you ultimately decide, you can pretty much expect your co-authors, the paper's editor and referees to wield the scientific axe, or ask for something extra to be included. I am still amazed by just how few of my amassed results made it into my first couple of papers. So be very selective – only directly relevant stuff gets in. Accept the idea that what existed as a whole section in your head might end up as a single sentence on the page. Also, the fact that you almost killed yourself getting a particular result doesn't automatically qualify it for inclusion.

Before starting to write, prepare all the figures and tables. These are, after all, the crux of the paper; without them in front of you, you can't really expect to write a thing. Make labelling unbelievably clear and simple. Nothing should be remotely ambiguous. Get as much of the incidental text as possible out of the main text and into methods and the legends; stuff like what the control experiments showed. Just include the nuts and bolts of the results in the main text, leaving the reader free to either refer to the extra detail, if they are interested, or to read on if they are not. This way, your manuscript will flow more smoothly. Remind yourself constantly that writing your results section simply means describing what your figures and tables show, nothing more. Assume nothing; explain everything. Remember, you are the expert. No one knows as much about your work as you! Write in short simple sentences that someone new to English could understand.

Writing the introduction before the discussion helps you to focus on where your research fits into the grand scheme of things. It's also extremely useful to keep rereading your introduction when writing the discussion. This helps you to avoid leaving gaps in your story or, worse still, contradicting yourself. This is not your end-of-year report (see Chapter 4); your introduction should be terse and to the point. Limit yourself to the literature that is strictly relevant.

Most other scientists will be far more interested in what they think your results mean than in what *you* think they mean. However, your discussion is a very important part of the paper. It's your chance to argue in favour of your results. If you really believe that what you've written is accurate (if not, I wouldn't want to be in your shoes), you'll want your readers to accept your conclusions as well as your results. Beware: it's easy to overstate your conclusions and make unconscious leaps of faith. After stinging criticism from my boss, I learned that the discussion is not the place to get excited. Sobriety and open-mindedness are the order of the day. Try to discuss all reasonable explanations and, if in any doubt, err on the side of playing down your conclusions and letting your results speak for themselves. Never forget that, in the first instance, you are writing for your editor and referees. These people don't suffer fools gladly.

Getting feedback on your paper

Once you've managed to write your first draft, you've overcome the hardest part. After all, the remainder of the process is about making the changes that other people suggest (or tell you to do). Without delay, forward your manuscript to your boss and encourage him or her to plaster your electronic draft in red font. As an inexperienced author, you need their critical input. My boss made comments such as, 'You can't make that assertion; it isn't really supported by your results.' To which a typical reply from me would be, 'Oh, isn't it? I thought it was!' Another classic from my boss, all too often repeated, was 'Do you really mean: "this result clearly shows that. . .", or merely "this result may suggest that . . ".'

35

After you've processed the great swathes of red typeface from your boss, and sought approval on the next draft(s) of your manuscript, next in line come your other co-authors. Naturally, they must all have the chance to read and make comments on the manuscript before it is submitted. Even minor authors can pick out irregularities that the bigwigs don't spot. Handling distant co-authors can be a lot harder than popping into the next office. Along with my boss, one foreign co-author and I spent a very long and exhausting time trafficking half-written drafts between us in what seemed like an eternal triangle. What's more, this person actually *was* a co-author – one who wrote a small chunk of the paper as well as approving my sections. Just exchanging intact figures (as large e-mail attachments or by FTP) added an extra dimension of difficulty. To reduce file size PDFs are by far the best bet; get yourself the full version of Adobe Acrobat® (adobe.com/products/acrobat/main.html).

As your career advances, you'll get much faster at writing papers. I have been known to get a first draft manuscript ready in only seven days. It's about cutting corners where you know you can and sussing when it's appropriate to rely on your co-authors. For my first paper, I tried hard to send a flawless manuscript to my collaborators for their approval. Needless to say, I didn't. Now I have learned that it is more efficient to send no more than the figures, along with a draft manuscript full of notes explaining what I meant, queries on suitable references, and requests for gaps to be filled. This first draft is also about you, the first author, deciding on the feel of the piece. This all saves you time and brings forward the date of receiving first feedback from your co-authors. This feedback is the fire that refines the paper, burning up the chaff that inevitably accumulates when you write something detailed and complex on your own. Never forget that objectivity decreases exponentially with increasing solo effort. In other words, you waste more time and achieve less the longer you plough on without external input.

Don't waste time perfecting the alignment of each panel in a figure until you know the figure is approved to stay in the final draft. Similarly, leave the completion of your reference list and the writing of your abstract until later (see below in this chapter). All you want at the first stage is to make sure you and your co-authors agree on what will form the skeleton of your article. So, if you have any specific requests, target particular co-authors by using coloured fonts at the relevant points in the text. Input from your more-experienced and better-connected co-authors is particularly invaluable in the discussion. They usually extract more scientific juice from the pulp of my unexplained results than I would ever think possible.

Finally, before you submit, get as many well-informed people as you can to read the manuscript. I try to pick one completely uninformed friend who can usually only understand three words out of every five. Uncluttered by the incomprehensible science, this individual can often spot the glaringly obvious error.

Getting your paper published

From first draft to final acceptance, getting your scientific paper published can take months, if not longer. Once you've written your paper with a specific journal in mind, and got it approved by all of your co-authors, you are ready to submit. Then the fun really starts. The 'Instructions for authors' page on your chosen journal's website can contain a formidable list of very specific requirements, almost 'picky' in its exactness. Failure to comply precisely with any one of these points could lead to rapid un-reviewed rejection of your manuscript; an abstract longer than the specified number of words, for instance, or a reference list in the wrong format. To check that you've got it all hunky-dory carefully peruse several recent papers from your chosen journal. Poorly written papers are often returned without even being reviewed, so pay a great deal of attention to whether your English makes sense. I take my hat off to non-native speakers who manage to write their science in clear, concise, and unambiguous English. It's not easy!

Next, turn your attention to your figures. If you've never printed them out until this point, you may get a shock when you do. They don't always turn out like the image you can see on your computer screen. Never waste too much time optimising your figures on screen until you've seen what the end product looks like. Even if you are submitting your paper online, you should check your printed figures. Remember, the journal's editors and typesetters decide on the final size of your figures, not you. Lest some unseen hand shrinks your figures, look at them once more to make them as bold, plain, and simple as you can.

Once you are happy with your final, no I mean really final, final draft, compose a covering letter to the editor, on behalf of your boss if he or she is the 'corresponding author'. It's quite legitimate to use the covering letter as an opportunity to stake a claim for the importance of your work, and suggest your preferred reviewers. You can also mention anyone you'd like not to review your work, a scientist working in a directly competing group, for instance. Try to sell your paper to the editor in glowingly understated terms.

Electronic online submission is now customary for most, if not all, top journals. This saves you the hassle of printing out several copies and then relying on snail-mail. What's more, there's often a facility for you to track the seamless progress of your paper as it cruises unhindered through the peer-review process. You wish! To submit electronically, you'll need to register yourself on the journal's Web page. They usually send you a page proof of your manuscript converted into a single PDF file. Needless to say, read this carefully before you click 'Submit'. It's your last chance to change your mind.

After an interminable few weeks of waiting, the referees' reports will finally arrive. It is fascinating, if nerve-racking, to read the opening paragraphs, where each referee summarises what they think your paper says.

The covering letter from the editor, will hopefully say that all the reviewers agree the paper makes a novel and important contribution that is of interest to the journal's readership and should be published. Even if it does, they may ask for changes to the figures, some more experiments, a few typos to be corrected, and revised interpretation of some of the results. This really is not atypical for a positive response. Think yourself lucky. Things could be much worse. You are, however, now under pressure. After all, you are usually only given a few weeks to respond with an amended manuscript. Drop everything: you have a golden opportunity. If you miss the window, you'll have to start the submission process all over again.

The editor often draws particular attention to some of the referees' comments. You must respond to these points to have any chance of getting your revised manuscript accepted. Though the implication is that responding to the other comments is not as crucial, don't risk it. Try to take account of most of them. The friendliest referees write orderly numbered comments: these are easy to deal with one at a time. It's hard work deciphering long pieces of prose to pick out specific points.

To get through this pressurised process, draw up a hit list of points merged from all the referees' and the editor's comments. First deal with the typos and any easily changed sentences. These amendments often only take an hour and greatly encourage you that you can meet the deadline. Then crack on with any additional experiments and make what other amendments you see fit. Remember that you have licence to argue against any suggested changes. Indeed, I once met a scientist who didn't make any of the substantive changes asked for by a key referee. He just argued his case, explained where the referee had misunderstood what he'd meant or done, and eventually got his paper accepted, virtually unaltered. To be on the safe side, make sure you respond in some way to each point, if only to make it clear why you did not think the criticism was valid.

Even though you might heave a sigh of relief once the final letter of acceptance arrives, it still isn't quite over. A few weeks later you'll have to check and correct a final proof of the paper. The turnaround at this stage is rapid, maybe only 24 hours to provide any minor corrections. After all those changes, it can be a little unnerving to wave bye-bye to the last chance to tinker with the odd word.

Stand in awe of those diligent scribes who go through this entire process three or more times before finally getting their work accepted. It can be a relentless battle.

Your paper might not make a big splash, but once its place in history is secure you will doubtless feel a great sense of peace – it has finally been laid to rest.

Abstract writing

As scientists, the most widely read words we'll ever write are our abstracts. Hopefully for years to come, stressed out final-year undergraduates all around the globe will be referring to your work in their dissertations based almost entirely on these short paragraphs. Once or twice during my fleeting but happy days as an undergraduate, we were passed a paper with the abstract blotted out, the object being for us to have a go at writing one. At the time I remember finding this task immensely difficult. I must have stared at the blank computer screen for an age before I stumbled on the way to attack these puzzles. The trick for me was learning that most of the important stuff in papers goes into the first and last sentences of each paragraph or section (see Chapter 3). Although I first read this in a cheap paperback book on how to bluff your way with speed-reading, I have put it into practice and more often than not it is true. Armed with this knowledge, I soon extracted the juice from the 'beheaded' paper by topping and tailing each section. Then I simply rewrote bits of the selected sentences (to get around that plagiarism thing), and the abstract simply self-assembled before my eyes. OK, OK, so my tutor said it was a bit stilted to read, but he had to admit that I hadn't missed a single salient point. Three years later I was charged with a different and more onerous task: to write the abstract to my first, first-author paper (see above in this chapter). Not knowing where to start I tried the same technique, but I was no longer happy to write anything that might be called stilted. So I concentrated on writing the thing in one smooth, flowing movement and realised that for this you need to know what you are writing about inside out, which explains why I couldn't do it as an undergraduate. Now it flowed, but I was no longer confident that I'd included everything. To get around this problem, I scanned through my results section to pick out the highlights, cross-checking the abstract to make sure I hadn't undersold my story. And suddenly there it was: all the salient points linked in a flowing style. It's amazing how presenting your paper in a nutshell makes the real worth of your discovery shine.

Perhaps the ultimate condensation challenge is writing your thesis abstract. I found the sheer quantity of information I needed to summarise into 200 words rather daunting. As the only criterion you can use to assess what to include is relative importance, you have to accept that six months hard graft may have to be turned into four words, or that some results are to be lost forever in the depths of Chapter V.

Writing an abstract for a conference is a different matter altogether. Like a poster (see Chapter 7), this sort of abstract is an advertisement for your work, not a peer-reviewed piece. Despite your secret desire to put people off coming to your talk or visiting your poster lest they ask awkward questions, you should seek to attract a big audience. On the other hand, you don't want to make your abstract so juicy that you either give away all your secrets in advance or commit to something you're not sure about. This is especially true if you have to submit your abstract months before the meeting. The best way around this is to leave your readers hanging at the end of the abstract, waiting for the talk to fill in the punch line.

Whatever type of abstract you have to tackle, the following simple structure should provide a good starting point:

1 Write a sentence or two briefly presenting the system you work on and possibly the essence of the knowledge to date. You can't summarise the entire introduction; you just need to encapsulate the state of play before your paper came along. Make it absolutely clear what you did and what other people did, for example by using phrases such as, 'It has previously been shown that . . .' and 'Here we tested . . .'

2 Summarise, in a sequence broadly similar to that of your results section, what your findings are, making sure you refer to the techniques you used. It's the difference between writing, 'We further showed that X is dependent on Y' and writing, 'Paramagnetic bipolar tolography revealed that X was dependent on Y.' This section should form the bulk of the Abstract, so cram as many keywords as possible in there, as the five or so additional keywords that journals allow you to specify will soon get used up.

3 Finally, state in the most succinct and descriptive terms exactly what your results mean: 'These results provide evidence that . . .' If you and your co-authors really believe you have shown something new, then be bold and claim it. Far more people will read this claim than will ever assess your evidence for it by reading the full text of your paper.

7

Conferences and
poster presentations

Conferences: a typical scenario

It's 7 a.m. and I'm in a strange bedroom. I know I have to get up
to face a very large free breakfast and a long first full day at my
chosen conference. My colleagues from the lab are in rooms
down the hall. When I left them in the bar last night they were
getting in the next round of drinks, so I don't expect to see them
much before lunch. Still, I have a busy day of networking ahead
of me, and I have a plan to help me extract the maximum value
from my conference. After I left the bar last night, I took a
highlighter pen to my newly acquired book of abstracts. At
least I now know which talks I want to see this morning. I will
go through this afternoon's sessions during the morning break,
and then this evening I can try to make my selections for the
remainder of the week.

It's now 9 a.m. and I'm sitting wide-eyed in a vast conference
room waiting for the first speaker. It's interesting how some
people seem to sit through whole sessions while others flit
from talk to talk in different lecture theatres and seminar
rooms. I've always found too many different interesting things
in the programme to take the former approach. You can never
predict what you will hear about in advance – in the past, some
of my best ideas have come from sitting in on talks on seemingly
unrelated topics. But this approach means I now have to 'leg it'
at top speed down a very long corridor to get to my next talk. I'll

doubtless be repeating this feat often during the week ahead. This is all very exciting, but equally stressful. The only consolation is that it gives me something to aim for. The prospect of spending my whole day in the same seat fills me with a sense of dread. During talks I tend to jot down a few keywords below the relevant abstract. This way I don't have to write down all the names and titles. I'm not a meticulous note keeper and I need time to absorb the visual impact of a presentation.

Hold on! What did they just say? It's now 3.30 p.m. and my ears have pricked up during a talk that I almost talked myself out of sitting through. The speaker just cast a ray of light into the very heart of my research. I have to speak to this person to find out more. I bolt down a quick coffee at the next break and spot 'my' speaker in a small crowd of people. There's a short queue waiting to get in before me, but I hover persistently. At last my chance arrives and I move in for a chat. With the briefest of introductions, we are up and running. We only have time for the barest of detail, but I've made contact. Perhaps I see a glimmer of excitement in their eyes when I tell them about my work. This person is now at the top of my list of new contacts to e-mail when I get home. On this occasion, I decide not to suggest a social meeting over lunch. They've said they'll track me down at the poster session and I don't want to come across as being pushy. I'm not desperate.

It's the evening of the second full day and I am at the poster session. These events are the best way to get around lots of different people quickly. I've already used a couple of breaks to scout around the poster hall in advance. This way I've been able to have a good look without crowds of people hanging around. I've made a list of all the poster numbers that I want to take a longer look at and any that I specifically want to speak to the author about. I remember to keep an eye out for the inevitable late arrivals – someone always puts their poster up very late. On arrival at this conference I tried to cross-reference my selected talk abstracts with my poster abstract 'targets'. You'll get much more out of a poster if you've heard any accompanying talk as well, and vice versa. During lulls in the evening, I stop 'camping out' at my own poster and make a beeline to the people I want to see. I have to repeat my little tour several times to make contact with as many people on my list as possible. It's a shame that some authors don't even bother to turn up for poster sessions. They are probably to be found in the bar! If only I knew what they looked like. At least I've managed to keep the time I have to spend away from my own poster to a minimum. I don't want to miss any potential 'customers', least of all my new contact! If I missed them, I'd miss their feedback and their fresh ideas.

It's the day after the poster session and I'm wandering around the trade exhibition. I spot a very unlikely looking character sitting behind one of the stands. Many people seem to have a subconscious rule to never talk to people sitting behind a desk at conferences. They must be trying to sell you something, right? Well that may often be true, but even trade exhibitors may still have information that could help you. I dive in for a quick chat and walk away ten minutes later with a few ideas to ponder, an offer of a free trial kit and a nice selection of freebies!

It's 10.30 p.m. on the penultimate day. All this networking has tired me out. My colleagues from the lab have decided to burn the midnight oil in the bar as well as attempting 'full-on' days of listening to talks. They are guaranteed to return home absolutely wrecked and in no state to do any work. Worse still, they'll probably doze off during one of the talks they especially want to hear. I make a rule to go easy on myself and set aside some time not only for sleep, but also for relaxation. I sometimes decide to hop on a bus to get away from it all for some good old retail therapy. Later, back in my room, I might read a novel or watch some junk TV. This time off pays rich dividends, as I am rested and alert in the morning.

I should add one quick word on conference food. It may be good or it may be bad, but it's been paid for. So resist the temptation to over indulge in cooked meals – there's nothing more sleep inducing than a big lunch followed by a traditional pudding with custard. I speak from experience. Go for the salad!

Of course, conferences come in many different forms, sizes, and locations and you are unlikely to experience one exactly like the one I've just described. But, whatever your first few conferences are like, you will probably face them feeling like an outsider looking in and this can sometimes make it hard to identify and make contact with key people. As they are the stage on to which you must force yourself if you are ever going to get noticed, you must overcome your stage fright and be bold. The more effort you put in, the more you will get out.

It's often quite easy to find financial assistance to attend conferences if you are a Ph.D. student or in your first post-doc. This often takes the form of travel grants and subsidised registration fees. You can often also get travel money or free registration by volunteering to help at a meeting. This also gives you an inside view of how conferences work. Check out the web site of the organising body for details.

Poster presentations

When telling non-scientist friends how much you enjoyed making your new poster, expect them to look rather puzzled. I too have suffered some very subdued reactions and now believe that most people think a poster is only a worthy undertaking for an elementary school project on 'Life in Our Pond'. The truth is that posters form an intrinsic part of scientific life. They're an advertisement for your research and a seriously effective way to get yourself noticed early in your career. You need to grab the attention of complete strangers as they may end up being your collaborators, best critics, generators of Ph.D.-saving ideas, or even your future employer.

Head up your poster with a short and informative title. It may be hard for people unfamiliar with your field to tell if they should bother to read your poster, so your title should arouse as much general interest as possible. If your project has a long-winded title, scrap it and write something punchy. Back up your title with an eye-catching summary. Make you message abundantly clear to your readers with short, punchy bullet points. Don't simply reproduce your abstract (see Chapter 6). At most conferences, delegates will already have a book of abstracts, so why waste precious poster space including it again? Distilling your abstract down to a single simple message will also help you get the knack for recognising exactly what your message is. This skill is absolutely fundamental to selling yourself. As far as the rest of the content goes, as long as you explain your key results really well and say what you are planning to do next, the rest is up to you. Don't be afraid to be selective – you don't have to include everything.

So, what overshadows good content and makes a poster 'look' bad? The next time you are at a conference try 'cruising the boards' to spot some common poster howlers. The most painful error is the inclusion of paragraph after paragraph of mind-numbingly boring text. Let's be frank, if they're *that* interested, they'll ask for your detailed materials and methods. You may be convinced that key workers in your field will want all this detail. But, are you sure even they will be bothered to read it all? If not, why include it? The brain tends to dismiss blocks of indigestible text, so dream up new ways to say it with a picture or diagram. Where you can't avoid using words, cut to the chase and use short bullet points. These are all good skills to acquire in today's fast-paced world. Learn to be inventive and be very critical of what you create. Just remember how billboard advertising gets its message across using minimal words and strong images – it's a multimillion-pound business for a very good reason. These advertising people are clever, but not that clever. If your poster is merely a scientific paper stuck up on a board, it'll have little impact.

The phrase 'Future work' is often seen at the bottom of postgraduates' posters. Let's face it, what this really means is, 'I may get to this one day if I'm lucky.' I soon wised up and now use the alternative 'Current work' on my posters, even if I am only going to start the work sometime in the next few weeks. 'Current' just sounds more convincing that you are on the ball experimentally, whereas 'Future' makes it abundantly clear that you haven't even started work on it yet. Thinking about little details like this can help to turn a defensive poster into an assertive one. You don't want your best idea for a future experiment pinched by your competitors because they don't believe you'll ever get around to it. Be bullish about what you plan to do.

Once you have your content in place, it is important to create a visually appealing poster. Now is the time to check the dimensions of the conference poster boards. Make sure your poster won't encroach on to your neighbour's board or leave its bottom hanging in mid-air. If you can, create your poster layout with a good presentations software package, like Microsoft Power-Point® (office.microsoft.com). Each section of your poster should be a separate panel, but don't cram the panels full of facts. Leave big margins, 15 mm say, around your boxes and 40 mm around the perimeter of your poster. As those advertising executives say, 'white space sells'. And try to avoid gaudy colours and funny fonts. They can be fun to use, but they may be off-putting to more sober members of your community. Arrange the boxes so they tell a logical story. You can even number boxes if they make more sense in a particular sequence. The 'look' of your poster will also improve if the individual boxes are lined up correctly; bad alignment at the margins just looks 'wrong'. Developing an eye for these details will impress your audience.

Once you have the whole package assembled, print out a draft copy. Your computer-generated poster will look very different on the wall. What seems like a reasonably large font size on your computer screen may appear tiny when printed at poster size, particularly when it is viewed from a distance of one metre. Get as many people as you can to give you their first impressions.

Print the finished product off as a single sheet, and, if you can afford it, get it laminated. Your nearest print shop should be able to help you with this. Although critics rightly point out that single-sheet posters are 'one-offs' that can't be updated with new results, a big poster is almost always more impressive than separate panels hastily assembled on the day. It's worth the extra money to give your poster that professional look. At your next conference be honest with yourself about how amateur any other kind of poster looks.

Finally, once you are at the conference, get your poster up early. It's your advertisement, so sell yourself! After all your hard work getting your poster just right, the scientists who spot it on the Tuesday lunchtime should be so impressed that they remember to search you out for a chat at the poster session on Thursday evening. By then, you should be camped out by your work of art 'touting for business'.

Figures 1 and 2 are a visual guide to good and bad poster design, respectively.

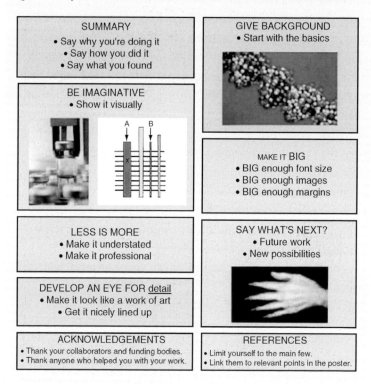

Fig. 1. Good poster design. Additional points: use one or two complementary but understated colours. Keep text to a minimum.

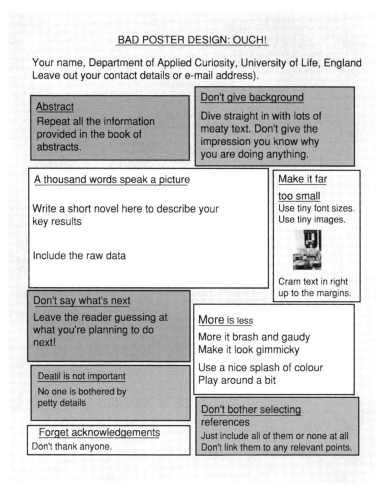

Fig. 2. Bad poster design. Spot the deliberate mistakes.

8

Writing and defending your thesis

Writing your thesis

I defy anyone to argue that there's an easy way to write a Ph.D. thesis. OK, so you can be organised and efficient about it, but, as far as I'm concerned, a Ph.D. isn't the top qualification without good reason. For me, the 'good reason' is the very process of constructing the thesis. Unless you are a natural born writer, it can be a bit of a slog.

After three years of hard work, and with the prospect of a salary only a couple of months away, I remember feeling a little radical towards my own thesis. So, I decided to break all the rules. I tackled the whole thing in one go, a sort of shotgun approach to thesis writing. Whilst perhaps unorthodox, I found this method extremely satisfying and very effective. The basic idea is to touch everything – every result, every paper – once and only once. You pick it up, look at it, make a decision and slot it right in where it needs to go. The object is to clear those piles of paper relatively quickly and get everything in electronic format as fast as possible. Once everything, and I mean everything, is on disk the battle is half won.

First, crack on with your figures and tables. Taking them each in turn, describe exactly what results you've got. You can use these descriptions as your figure and table legends, and a bit later on as the basis for your results sections. Use a similar approach to tackling the literature. Distil out what you've picked up from each paper – a short sentence is often all you need – and slot it into place. It seems that a little of this spade-work goes a long way. Just lump relevant bits of text together and sort them out when you eventually get back to attacking that section. It's crude but effective.

Lest you find yourself procrastinating over how to subdivide each lump into smaller and smaller sections, please just get writing. You'll like yourself much more when you've started on this journey. Kick it off by tackling something familiar. If you've written a paper before, so much the better; paste chunks of it straight in where you need it. You'll soon forget any high ideals of starting to write it all from scratch. Anything you have previously written – even if unread by anyone except yourself – is now precious. Just chop it up, sort out the chaff, and use it, even if you only manage to salvage a single sentence. Sometimes you'll find that a sentence written in the unhurried days of your first year is a pure gem of insight.

This shotgun approach demands that you have six or more files open simultaneously on your computer screen, so it helps if you have a fast computer with auto-save switched on. If you don't, you'll soon forget which files you haven't recently saved. With words and pictures flying into so many different files, backup your work frequently. The thought of losing even one day's work made up of so many unconnected bits is not worth thinking about.

The cardinal sin for all budding thesis writers is to deal with too much detail too soon. It's so very easy to get sidetracked by trivia. Figures, especially, have a way of sucking you in. Before you know what's happened, you've effectively wasted four or five hours of good writing time faffing around trying to get one figure nicely lined up and labelled. The counterargument goes, 'you have to do it some time, so surely it's all to the good'. I disagree for two reasons. First, why seek to attain perfect figures that you or your boss will probably later amend or scrub altogether? Second, the more you kid yourself that what you're doing is useful work, the harder it'll be to get writing properly. OK, so you may experience a premature sense of triumph once you've finally converted your carefully selected results into figures and tables, but they are just the beginning, and the easiest bit. Soon comes the dawning realisation that the toughest meat of your thesis is not your results themselves, it's what you say about them.

The biggest potential pitfall of the shotgun writing method is never finishing anything. Don't think this approach to thesis composition means doing the writing quickly. That's a recipe for shoddy work. You might spend an hour or more on one quite short section, but the point is to finish what you start, even if it's only a single paragraph. This way you don't have to waste time rereading what you only half-wrote two weeks ago. Naturally, to make this work you have to have faith in what you've already written.

This fast-track approach does, however, have the advantage of enabling you to maintain your interest in the whole endeavour. If you have to spend ages stuck on one section, because that's the only bit you have on the go, you might soon lose inspiration. As a shot-gunner you just finish off the paragraph, open another file, and move on to a totally different area. A change really is as good as a rest. I wrote for hours on end by periodically chopping and changing like this.

If you are methodical, you'll eventually reach a point when you have gathered together an incomplete but critical mass of text in each section. When you recognise this point, it instantly becomes time to kill off your thesis chapter by chapter. Warn your boss well in advance of the impending deluge of first drafts.

The shotgun strategy might not suit everyone. Some will find the long wait until the first finished chapter just too freaky. But, if you are up for it, you might just find that the long, dark rite of passage called your thesis write-up isn't quite the endurance test you first thought.

The final thesis defence or *viva voce* examination

There are two ways to approach your final thesis defence, or *viva voce* examination. One is to see it as something that has to be got through or, dare I suggest, simply survived. The other is to attack it in an upbeat and confident manner with the attitude that nothing is going to stop you convincing your examiners that you and your work are worthy of the degree. How you get on will depend partly on what sort of confidence trick you can play on yourself before you go through that fateful door into the examination room. The remainder of your performance depends, of course, on how well you know your stuff, but more on that later.

You may be under the impression that a Ph.D. is really some kind of long-service award. Surely, if you've made it through to the end, then you're all but guaranteed to get the degree. EERGH-EERGH. (Please imagine the embarrassing sound that accompanies an incorrect answer in a TV quiz show.) WRONG! I've personally come across two cases where the candidate failed to get their Ph.D. on the day. No, I really do mean failed; not just candidates who were asked to resubmit, or asked to go back to the lab and produce more work, or even, perish the thought, offered a master's degree.

Both of these total failures (the theses, not the candidates, I mean) were axed by the same thesis examiner, who, under the UK examination system, had read and appraised the work. I know him well, and he's not an unkind person. The most sobering insight I gained was when he told me that one of these candidates would have to put up a truly outstanding performance on the day to stand a chance of getting anything out of it. Needless to say, they didn't. Apparently, words like 'lacked confidence', 'confusing', and 'apathetic' were used. Ouch! So much effort for no reward; I can't imagine how they felt. The message: Don't assume anything, good or bad, when approaching your big day. It's still all to play for. In the UK, you can strongly suggest choices to your Ph.D. adviser about who your thesis examiner is, although you cannot make any kind of approach to them   55 yourself. If you have a choice, choose someone who will really test you without being unfair.

If you take a *'viva* survival' attitude, your final thesis defence is likely to be, well, less than rigid – and you'll probably have at least some doubt about the outcome. If you are feeling mentally worn out after years of academic toil, it is all too easy to take the view, 'I'll just leave it up to the examiners to decide if my thesis is good enough.' But, with this attitude, you are actually making it much harder for them to decide which box to tick on the examiners' report form. Any doubt in their minds reduces your chances that the tick will be in your favour.

The name of the game is putting in a performance that bolsters any cracks in your written work and makes it hard for your examiners to tick the boxes lower down the list. I'm talking about those nightmarish boxes with long, dark names like: 'that no degree be awarded and permission be not granted to resubmit in revised form but that the candidate be offered the degree of master instead'. Here is a brief five-point plan to becoming a *'viva* thriver' not just a *'viva* survivor':

1 **Be confident**. You are more of an expert than they are.
2 **Know your thesis inside out**. Imagine you are preparing evidence for a legal defence in court.
3 **Be scholarly**. You are asking to be let into the inner circle of your scientific community.
4 **Stick to what you do know**. All other ground is quicksand.
5 **Ask questions**. Appear keen to fill in gaps in your knowledge.

You are a novice scientist. In stark contrast, your thesis examiner is not. What's more, he or she knows your subject inside out and will spot every single error or omission that you have made in your thesis.

Not!

OK, let's address some of the major misunderstandings here. First, you are more of an expert than they are. You did the work and you wrote the thing. So, think of yourself as holding all the cards. If you can argue your point well, they'll just have to accept what you say. Imagine that they are questioning your choice of experiment, and asking why an alternative approach wasn't adopted. Your response might be, 'I considered trying that method but the necessary equipment wasn't available in the department, and I didn't have the opportunity to go elsewhere to do the experiment.' Since they weren't there at the time, what else can they come back at you with? Point won. The truth is, one of the main things your examiners are trying to pin down is whether you can deal with criticism and argue your case in appropriate scientific language. If it appears that you know your thesis inside out (and, by now, you should) and you can give a good account of why you did what you did, you are already a long way to winning your examiners over. The other thing they will want to check out is whether you can think on your feet to produce a well-reasoned response to an unexpected question. In other words, are you scholarly?

Second, they most certainly will not spot all your howlers. You may be thinking, 'How could I have missed that?' But realise that your Ph.D. advisor also missed it. And, if both you and your advisor can miss a howler, anyone can. So, expect a list of minor corrections from each of your examiners. I spotted what was, for me, a major howler in my thesis. Neither examiner noticed it, so I quietly corrected it before submitting my bound thesis to the library.

Earlier I alluded to the idea that you might be able to bypass gaps in your knowledge during your final thesis defence. There are several ways you can try to do this. The first approach is to bluff.

DO NOT BLUFF!

If you make out that you know about something that you don't, make no mistake, you will eventually be caught out. A legitimate alternative, as practised by all the best scientists and politicians, is to gloss over gaps in your knowledge by turning the discussion back to what you want to talk about so you can demonstrate how much you do know. Acknowledge the areas you know only a little about as they pop up (lots of nodding and eye contact) then keep going back on to safer ground. This assertive behaviour will go down well, as your examiners will see you doing what they do all the time: intellectual swordplay.

If you feel you've impressed and clocked up enough points, you can even let yourself ask your examiners to explain something to you. This has a two-fold spin-off. First, they'll naturally feel glad to talk about their own area of expertise. Second, your openness in admitting you don't know something will leave your examiners with the useful impression that the rest of the time you knew exactly what they were on about (even if you did not).

Once it's all over, relax and brace yourself for the inevitable anticlimax. There's a lag period before the real fun starts at the graduation ceremony!

9

Coping with pressure and stress

It's hard to forget the first time you experience jaw-clenching pressure. I thought I had experienced the true meaning of pressure during my undergraduate finals. But I realised I was wrong when I first encountered real pressure near the end of my Ph.D. I had just six weeks to finish all my lab work. That's when I learned that there was another dimension of pressure that I still had to probe. When I met the real McCoy it left me physically short of breath. It was the kind of pressure that leaves you shaking inside, even though you try all the relaxation tricks you know.

So what plunges someone into this kind of cul-de-sac of stress? And, once you have driven down it, how do you manage to reverse out of 'stress alley'? It is not a nice place to be. In recent years the 'stress screw' has been turned more tightly in all professions. Everyone now has targets and deadlines, and we all have our own personal league table to try to clamber up. Coupled with this, job security, by and large, doesn't exist anymore. OK, that's enough bleakness. You didn't buy this book to top up on depressive stories. You want advice to encourage and uplift you, so let me perform a little analysis of what I went through.

The truth is, I'm not 100% certain why I let myself get in such a state to start with. But stress is like that; it slowly creeps up on you unannounced and then one day goes in hard and grabs you from behind. This was an extraordinarily busy time for me, both in and out of work. My social life and voluntary work were both piled high, whilst at work things had never been more frantic. We all have a threshold beyond which we genuinely freak out. Although we see stress as the enemy, it may just be a safety valve that warns us to stop before we hit serious trouble. I, for one, am glad that my threshold is set no higher than it is.

During one week alone I was trying to get a paper out, write a review, and move forward with my back-to-back grant and fellowship applications. This was on top of routine stuff such as presenting my work at a seminar, supervising a postgraduate student in the lab, whilst going ahead full throttle with my own experiments, not to mention a dozen or so minor inconveniences such as several assorted meetings to attend. It was utterly insane. If I were working this hard in advertising, I would have had my own team of people and an annual salary far beyond what I'm likely to earn in the next four or five years put together.

Ph.D. students and post-docs are particularly vulnerable when it comes to stress. I know some principal investigators (PIs) reading this will argue that, 'You ain't seen nothing yet,' but I plead extenuating circumstances on three counts. First, in real terms, you guys have already made it: you've been rated highly enough to get a permanent job. So, even though the pressure's still on you to perform, the pressure to find your own salary every three years is now off. I have a sneaking feeling that a little more security would go a long way to chilling younger scientists out.

Second, PIs are used to stress, whilst graduate students, especially, are not. When I was suffering badly at the wrong end of 'stress alley', I was experiencing pure culture shock. My mind and body had never taken this kind of punishment before. At the height of my stress, I just wanted to be an undergraduate again – at least for a week or two's convalescence. Third, and most importantly, students (and post-docs especially) have to be full-time experimental scientists on days when they could easily spend ten hours in front of their computers just like proper PIs.

For me, there is only one way to do a stress reverser. Just trying to relax and ignore it all is impossible; the stress comes to get me at night when I am asleep and I wake up, heart pumping. The way I see it, when stress comes a-knocking, I either have to quit my career or crack on with it. As the former isn't on my list of options, I'd better face up to the latter. The work isn't going to disappear unless I set about making it go away. So, my solution for stressed-out young scientists is twofold.

First, you need to work very hard. This is the easy bit. Second, you need to survive the onslaught of all this work. Avoid the danger of burning out by first throwing overboard anything and everything you possibly can that is superfluous. Focus solely on urgent, essential tasks. When faced with a seemingly infinite amount of work but a definitely finite amount of time, you have to cut corners where you can. Push on to complete individual tasks rather than spinning plates, because task completion makes your stress level come down a notch or two. Next, treat yourself to an easier life for the duration of your struggle. Eat out. Get to bed early as often as you can and, whilst you are there, sleep yourself silly. Plan your summer holiday. Just do anything that reminds you that there is a lot to enjoy out there and better times to look forward to.

A wise person once said to me, 'All things come to an end.' Eventually, the once seemingly impossible becomes possible. You will find yourself in calmer waters, reflecting with a wry smile on that crazy time back in the spring when you wondered why you ever went into science. I reckon all this stress is some bizarre rite of passage, organised by all PIs everywhere, to see if we underlings have what it takes to make it to the top. Don't let them see you beaten. Let's push on to the finishing post!

Unless you have a set-in-stone deadline to finish your lab work by, a Ph.D. can feel like a bad relationship – easy to get sucked into but difficult to end. Almost without realising it, you can find yourself drawn in by the magnetic power of the next experiment, and the one after that. But beware . . . under this spell you can lose the power of rational thought, and, as time goes by, you may even end up in a place that you can't, or won't let yourself, escape from: 'the laboratory of never-ending "last" experiments'.

But a Ph.D. is only of value to you as the springboard to your future career. You need to finish it, and that means drawing your lab work to a close and writing the thing up. Put bluntly, if you are approaching the end of your Ph.D. funding, you really do need to get out of the lab. For most people, writing up and lab work are mutually incompatible. This explains why PIs are often reluctant to offer post-doc positions to Ph.D. students who've not completed their theses.

The onus is on you to escape from the lab – don't wait for someone else to tell you that it's time to make the break. Ph.D. advisors are always seeking just one more 'key' result from you. So don't expect them to pull the plug on your research at an early enough stage for you to submit within your allotted number of years. If you want a barometer of when you have enough results for your thesis, they may be the last person you should ask. Consult someone else's advisor and ask them to be brutally honest with you. And, when you make the decision to stop work in the lab, stick to your guns. I had to say no to my boss several times before he got the message that I really wasn't going to do any more experimental work.

Getting to the point of saying a final 'no' requires a strategy. First write a hit list of final experiments. Your first draft of this list will probably be unachievably long. It would also, almost certainly, take you even more time to complete than you've estimated. So, before ploughing into your list, first ask yourself 'is my experiment really necessary?'. At least two of my essential final Ph.D. experiments, that somehow survived the initial cull, were eventually shelved: I just didn't need them for my thesis. The point is that I really believed I did. Talk to good post-docs and read their theses. This is a good way to avoid the delusion that you need to have attempted absolutely everything on your list before you submit. After all, you have plenty of leeway to argue, both in writing and orally, why you didn't do something (see Chapter 8). Best of all, describe how you made a conscious decision to do another more informative experiment instead of the one you left out. Prioritise your final hit list so you can knock off outstanding experiments in the order of their importance to your thesis. This way you always have the option of letting the stragglers drop off the end of your list if you run short of time, a bit like a newspaper editor chopping the end of a report one sentence at a time until it fits into the space on the page.

These final few weeks in the lab are the occasion to bring all your time management skills to bear (see Chapter 2). Make use of any gaps in your busy schedule to prepare for writing. To start with, sort out the chaff from your files and make one more back-up copy of everything essential. Do anything that might ease the pain of the impending write-up. Even if it's only the odd half-hour spent preparing one of your tables, it'll be worth it. When you come across these little titbits of effort in the middle of your write up, they'll give you a small, but probably much needed, boost. If you can't contain the urge to write, your best bet is to update your materials and methods chapter. If nothing else, this will help you to realise just how many techniques you've learnt. It is also essential to tackle this whilst you are still immersed in the laboratory with every source of information to hand.

So, now that you're raring to go with your pared down list of really crucial final experiments, crack on and get them sorted, once and for all. If you are already feeling run down after months and months of slogging it out day-in, day-out with Mother Nature, you'll need to tap into all your reserves for this final push. And, it's not as if you can look forward to a nice rest when it's all over. The whole point of the exercise is to get you writing up early. Perhaps an incentive is in order. I made plans to sneak off for a week's holiday between finishing in the lab and starting the big write-up. You'll never again find such a natural break point. Perhaps I should say 'breaking point' after that last mad rush in the lab! Planning a nice little trip away will give you something rewarding to aim for and, if travel tickets and accommodation bookings are involved, an unbreakable deadline.

PART III

The transition to post-doctoral research

10

From graduate student to post-doc

How I found my first post-doc job

At the end of the second year of my Ph.D., I began thinking about my first proper research job. I started by 'cold-mailing' a few project leaders to see what funding they might have in the pipeline. I just sent them a one-paragraph e-mail, selling, but not overselling, myself. This approach resulted in a range of responses: 'Contact me again in a few months' time'; 'Can you send me your resumé?'; 'You might like to apply for this job I'm advertising in September'; and, best of all, 'Perhaps you'd like to come and visit my lab'. OK, so they were far from offers of formal interviews, but what did I expect at this stage? Only time would tell whether these first contacts might lead to something more concrete later on. At least I'd got in early and hopefully made a positive impression. But, as it turned out, my first post-doc job didn't result from any of these tentative approaches, nor from any of the job advertisements in the scientific press. I was fortunate enough to secure my first job without ever having an interview. I created it myself. If this strikes you as unlikely, let me explain how I did it, and try to convince you that you too can have a crack at controlling your own fate.

1 **Step one: have an outstanding idea.** I had a really good idea for a project. To be honest, I just got lucky – hearing about an exciting new result when I was at a conference. The lucky bit is that I was at that particular session at all, and that I was paying attention at the crucial moment! Immediately, I recognised

that this finding had enormous implications for my own future research. I guess this is the 1% inspiration dear old Edison referred to. Like surfing, science is all about catching the big wave at the right time. I think someone was looking after me that day.

2 **Step two: find a project leader.** No funding body would give the money directly to me, a mere graduate student, more's the pity, so I had to find myself a potential project leader. I had already decided to move on from my current lab after my Ph.D. My advisor and I got on OK, I just didn't fancy the idea of another three-year stint in the same place, that's all. I was fortunate enough to meet an excellent alternative boss when visiting another university. Now, if only I could find a way to work with him! Gingerly, I sent off a short e-mail stating my idea in a nutshell and suggesting that we co-write a grant proposal. My cheekiness paid off. He loved the idea and thought it would stand a fair chance of being funded. A couple of weeks later we had a face-to-face meeting to hammer out the details of the proposal. He added lots of his own ideas. I didn't mind this at all – I knew I needed his input and streetwise approach if this grant was going to stand a chance of being funded. Once you start collaborating seriously (see Chapter 11), the input from other labs into your proposals becomes invaluable.

3 **Step three: apply for funding.** We decided to apply for funding from three very different sources. We knew that two of these applications were long shots. It was the third, most likely source, that in the end provided the funding. As it turned out, there were some other sources we could have tried for, but we never got around to writing more than three proposals. This wasn't just a case of making life easy on ourselves, we also knew that it's a 'no-no' in science to submit multiple applications simultaneously for exactly the same project. However, writing to three different funding bodies meant tailoring what we proposed to suit each case. I wrote the bulk of the two long-

shot grants myself, with my would-be boss doing the polishing and approval bit. He then wrote most of the third proposal, based largely on the other two. As any project leader will confirm, writing good fundable grant proposals takes a lot of attention to detail . . . and a lot of time. Writing my first grant proposal was like nothing I'd ever written before. I had to pin down specific, achievable aims and objectives, estimate how long it was going to take me to complete each stage, and how much it would all cost. I had to show that this project was all but guaranteed to make a significant new contribution to knowledge and that the work done would meet international standards. To make matters worse, all three of the application forms had different formats and a different set of requirements!

If I thought that writing the proposals was difficult, waiting for the response once they were submitted was even worse. The waiting lasted for months and was utterly interminable. I just tried to throw myself into my remaining Ph.D. research and forget about the applications. When the first two rejection letters eventually arrived, I became a little depressed. I knew that each application had taken the best part of two very long and intense weeks out of the tail end of my Ph.D. What's more, we weren't even short-listed for either application. I know that rejection letters are a fairly frequent occurrence for academics, but whereas these guys already have a permanent job, I felt that my whole future was resting on the outcome of my one remaining application. It didn't look good. I started to think a lot about the earlier groundwork that I'd done with other labs. At the time I was really glad I at least had the sniff of a fallback position. I kept on nurturing my other contacts right up until the final verdict.

4 **Step four: celebrate (hopefully).** In the end, all the effort paid off – we were funded! I found it a scary and humbling experience to realise that my initial idea had been funded to the tune of . . . well, it seemed to me like an awful lot of money. And it

69

was a wonderful feeling of relief to know that I had a job in the bag before I'd even started writing my thesis. What an incentive to crack on during the few remaining months and finish it off! So many people had already warned me about the dangers of writing up whilst working.

Having read about the amount of work involved, you may feel that you'd rather give all this a miss and wait for the job adverts to appear. After all, at least that way you know they've already got the money to hire you; all you have to do is compete for the job with a group of other people. But, for those of you who feel a little pushy, I'd urge you to give the grant-writing thing a go. Regardless of what doom-and-gloom stories you might hear, there is money out there to be won, even by would-be post-docs!

Starting out

As a pre-doc post-doc, you are the most contradictory of scientific employees, paid a proper scientist's salary, but without that crucial piece of paper that says you are a 'Doctor'. Even with the title 'Doctor' you may not instantly *feel* like a legitimate part of your scientific community. Perhaps the magnitude of the title is too great for you to take in just yet. Or maybe your Ph.D. years have desensitised you to the novelty of it all. Yet, despite the monstrous quantity of work you have shifted, getting to feel like a proper scientist can take a bit longer.

Once you are over the final hurdle of your Ph.D. steeplechase, you will probably sense a difference in the way your new peer group, the non-student scientific community, behaves toward you – a very positive difference. Once you are employed as a scientist an unspoken barrier drops: you feel as if you are 'in', so to speak. But whether all those lecturers, readers, and professors suddenly want to treat you as an equal out of respect, or merely feel obliged to do so, is open to debate. I like to think that this warm feeling of acceptance is the direct result of their seeing you emerge relatively unscathed from your Ph.D. Perhaps seeing someone finish imbues in others, who have tackled a Ph.D. in years gone by, a natural sense of camaraderie. It helps if you take your first post-doc job in a different part of the country, so none of these folk remember you as an incompetent, first-year Ph.D. Whatever the reason, it's nice to feel that, at the end of one of life's great challenges, you have managed to acquire just a little well-deserved kudos.

Alongside this new sense of belonging, there is also a slightly more worrying feeling. Some, at least, of the Ph.D. students in the lab might seem to regard you as the fountain of all wisdom. On many occasions you may be asked questions that you just haven't got a clue how to answer. What's more, if Ph.D. students imagine you know it all, then how much more will a fresh-faced undergraduate student expect? Naturally, your most pressing concern is the fear of making a complete and utter fool of yourself. We all know that science is a bad career choice for bluffers. To deal with this situation, opt for the humble approach. When asked about a technique you've never even tried, just come clean and admit defeat. As I see it, any alternative will leave you looking like an idiot sooner or later. I found that this open approach led to the number of unanswerable enquiries dropping off very quickly! Remember the old management consultant's adage, 'under-promise, over-deliver'. Who knows, if you can lower people's expectations a little, maybe you can show what you are capable of in your own time.

Unfortunately, though, during my first two weeks in the lab as a post-doc, I made the big mistake of being too successful: the couple of major steps forward I took turned out to be more of a curse than a blessing. You see, my new boss developed the habit of popping his head around the corner every hour to seek another update. Clearly, we were suffering from a very bad case of, 'What have you done since we last spoke?' It didn't take me too long to cotton on to the long-term implications of this situation. Even if I could sustain this level of output, which I sincerely doubted, there was just no way I could face this constant barrage

71

of enthusiasm. What my boss and I needed was a cooling off period. I set about consciously reducing contact time and offered 'nothing to report' when I did bump into him. This seemed to do the trick, although I may have overcooked things a little: for a while I got the distinct feeling he thought that I was a complete slacker. This all points back to the need to work at a sustainable pace – a good idea for any scientist.

Though moving to a fresh institution for my first post-doc job was a positive experience, I did miss the on-the-spot advice and support of my old scientific buddies. In my old stamping ground I'd accumulated some real gems – people who seemed to know just about everything no matter what you asked them. Now I was on my own and one of my first challenges was to start gathering my own little army of unofficial 'mentors' all over again. Although I still made use of my former friends, not to mention my old boss, e-mail or the telephone is no substitute for on-site help. Besides, I'm sure there's an unspoken limit to the number of questions one can fire at someone who isn't seeing you on a day-to-day basis. You could end up being thought of as a nuisance, or worse still, a hanger-on.

These repeated rounds of alliance building from scratch are part and parcel of the highly mobile post-doc life. First, realise just what a sociable business science is. The Golden Rule of 'do unto others as you would be done unto' is smack on here. You never know whose help you might need, so be good to everyone. In some ways I think the cleaners and porters are just as important to get on your side as the Head of Department. Second, rightly or wrongly, once you have finished your Ph.D., you might feel that the type of question you can ask is more restricted. As you've got all this assumed knowledge, you might find it nigh-on impossible to ask a question that, by now, you really should know the answer to. Let's face it, few of us come out of our Ph.D.s knowing everything that we should. You are probably now painfully aware that it won't be too long before you're the person being asked these same basic questions by a new and expectant face in the lab. A little extra effort in your Ph.D. sure goes a long way in your first post-doc job.

So, the take-home message for all you first-time post-docs is to enjoy your newfound status, but consider taking the pressure off yourself at the start of your job. After all, you've just finished a Ph.D. for goodness' sake! So cut yourself a little slack for the first few weeks at least – you've probably never had it so good!

Get yourself let in on science's secrets

In the aftermath of my final thesis defence I realised that I was no longer facing academic targets, only a long road of personal career development. To become a legitimate part of any community, you have to be let in on its secrets, and this is no different for scientists. Now you might think that there is some very rational way to get to know science's trade secrets. But, this is just not so. The seemingly structured career path that leads to research is a cover-up. There's a mass of absolutely vital information that you can only acquire by word of mouth – or bitter experience. Many academic institutions are making efforts to professionalise their postgraduate training schemes with mandatory courses on presentation skills and the like, and glossy ring binders packed with user-friendly course notes – but these efforts are unlikely to leave you feeling fully informed. All professions have their unwritten rules, but the very continuation of science seems to depend on scientists passing on to newcomers the secrets of how their profession works, through a complex network of informal contacts.

The peer-review process for grants and refereed papers is perhaps the prime example of a science secret. For instance, you need to get to grips with the finer points of what is, or is not, acceptable to write down without being (scientifically speaking) unprofessional. There is a fine line between making a 'jump-the-gun' statement and not exploiting your data to the full, with both possibilities offering easy paths to unprofessionalism. Try to get any potential *faux pas* in your writing pointed

73

out to you by someone friendly before you click the 'send' button (see Chapter 6).

So, in science, it's not so much a question of who you know as whom you obtain received wisdom from. Broadening and maintaining your network of contacts is the only way to tap into the constant flow of unwritten information that keeps the whole thing functioning. In practice, the missing information in your Ph.D. training scheme can only be filled by scraps gleaned from more experienced scientists whom you access on your own initiative.

Take my advice, accept just how quirky and intensely personal science really is and play along with it – it'll save you a lot of heartache. Some may argue that painful lessons are more likely to shape your scientific personality and lead to you finding out your own little secrets. This may be true, but, in my experience, painful lessons might also result in you unwittingly upsetting a lot of people along the way. And the last thing you want to get early in your career is an undeserved bad name for being a pain in the behind.

To get ahead in science you need to get yourself invited into the inner circle of established scientists. Science is a wonderful career for individualists, but a bad choice for loners. Scientists often find themselves portrayed in movies as isolated geeks, but a successful scientist in the real world certainly has to be a people person, make no mistake.

11

Collaboration and visiting other labs

To the uninitiated, it may not be obvious why someone in their first post-doc position would want to establish a collaboration with a scientist in another, perhaps distant, lab. Look at it from the point of view of your prospective future employer. They want to see a candidate who will be able to contribute to their scientific community; someone who can network successfully with their colleagues abroad, for instance. Get collaborating and you will be demonstrating the very skills required for getting on well in twenty-first century science. The tiny number of single-author research papers published these days is testimony to the need to collaborate.

That's all very well, but what's in it for you? Science can be very competitive, so you may be understandably reluctant to share your results or even draw attention to your presence in the field, at least until your work is in some shape to publish. Collaboration is all about efficiency – reducing the time taken to produce valuable results. Translated, that could mean that you might get to do the really interesting experiments that you never dreamed you'd have time to do before the end of your project. Even those you currently view as competitors can some-times become collaborators. The best example of this is where you have something they don't. Then you can start to bargain for access to what they have that you need, be it results, expertise, equipment, or whatever. Other potential collaborators may not even care what you are up to, but they may still have something priceless to offer you: they may have done some of your hardest work for you. Imagine you are faced with a seemingly insurmountable list of experiments (you may not have to stretch your imagination too far, I would guess!). Then you discover that someone from a large and wealthy group, who works in a related field, has just casually knocked off your most dreaded experiment. What took them two weeks might take you six months by the time you learn the technique from scratch. All you have to do is ask them nicely if you could have the result or end product. The perception amongst new scientists is 'there's no way they'll just give it to you'. Believe you me, they may well do just that. It's how science works. For the chance of a joint authorship, or even an acknowledgement on your paper, your fellow scientists will often gladly tell you their results or send you their stuff. The trick is to ask in a way that increases your chances of success, but more on that later.

In my experience, there are two sorts of collaboration. The first is where you bump into someone who is either working in your field or who is doing something that you think may be useful to you. At a conference 'bumping into them' may literally mean that – something jumps out at you from their poster or talk. In this case, you need to make a quick decision whether it's best to get talking face-to-face or wait to make first contact after the conference from the relative safety of your computer (see Chapter 7). As a general rule of thumb, I tend to jump right in with Ph.D. students and fellow post-docs, but I think twice before marching up to scary professors. Your advisor may also have 'issues' with senior scientists that you are not privy to, so speak to your boss first if you are in any doubt. As well as in person, you can also 'bump into' colleagues in the literature or via a Web search.

The second collaboration type is where you have identified a need to collaborate in advance of knowing who may be able to help you. This is harder to approach as the onus is on you to find the best person for the job. Without inside contacts and inside knowledge of your community (enter your advisor), this may come down to doing a bit of good old-fashioned detective work. The Web can be a lifesaver if your advisor can't help you, although you still need to ask around if you can once you have one or two people in mind.

In collaborations of either type, you will want to work with someone who will be open and fair with you. It's pointless throwing your results away in a one-way relationship. Imagine that you've decided to tell one or more potential collaborators that your piece of science might be of interest to their research. These people you've identified could well be working on the other side of the world. Unless you have already met them at a conference (in which case they may not remember you anyway), they have almost certainly never heard of you, or, quite possibly, your advisor's group. So, whoever they are, you will need to start by introducing yourself.

You could try cold-calling on the telephone, but chances are the people you are trying to contact are either at a conference, are in meetings with their own people, or are just too busy to want to speak to you. The good thing about using e-mail for first contact is that you are not pressuring the other people by demanding their immediate attention. The bad thing is that the other people can easily choose just to ignore you. And that's the first hurdle in getting collaborations off the ground. Busy, successful scientists can receive upwards of 50 e-mails a day, so, to ensure your message is even read, you need to get yourself noticed with an eye-catching subject line. Keep it very short, but make sure you include *their* keywords (XYZ); make it sound like something *they* will want to read. They probably don't want to hear about your results – they want to know what's in it for them. So, for example, you could use, 'Opportunity to collaborate with group working on XYZ.'

Once your message is opened, you face the next hurdle: convincing them that it's worth their while bothering to reply. So state your name and who you work for, then summarise the general area of your research in no more than two lines! If you

77

talk about yourself too much, they may well 'switch off' and start scanning down the page. Some more obvious issues: get to the point and keep it brief and state exactly what you would *like* from them (i.e., say '*please*'), not what you want. Give them numbered points to avoid misunderstandings.

But what happens if they don't reply after, say, a week? Well don't give up. I once sent three e-mails and made four phone calls trying to track down a possible collaborator. After almost giving up hope, I got a reply by e-mail that was full of apology for the delay and gave me exactly the news I had been hoping for. Some scientists really are unbelievably busy, even if they spend much of their time sitting in airport lounges. The above example was an extreme case, but I always remind myself to follow up with at least a second – and, if it's really important, a third – e-mail spread over the course of a month. This allows for absences due to conferences and other visits. The second time around, include your original message in case the first one got deleted. Be polite and simply restate your interest, rather than rudely asking if they have had the time to read your message. If all else fails, ring them or ring their lab and speak to someone who can help you get a message to them.

If you get lucky and receive a favourable reply (most people eventually respond well to a brief, intelligent request), talk to your boss before you respond. There are lots of people out there who'd like privileged access to your unpublished results, and your boss, not you, is the one person who should decide what detail, if any, you share with them. Thank goodness I have no personal experience of having my results 'scooped', but naïve souls have fallen foul of unscrupulous scientists saying 'thank you very much and goodbye' once they had picked off the information they wanted.

The politics of collaboration can be a daunting prospect for post-docs who haven't even met all the key players in their own immediate field. Your advisor must play a key role if you are to negotiate (literally, negotiate) your way through the subtleties of scientific protocol, especially because the nitty-gritty of this process will probably be carried out mostly via e-mail. Without access to the human voice and body language, this can all get a bit cagey, and it can certainly open you eyes to how much science – like any other profession – is all about personalities. If the other person is a bit of an unknown quantity, your boss may want to start by offering a small interesting titbit of information from your lab-book to see what is given in return. Or you could write a general statement about your work that catches the other party's interest but doesn't really tell any useful detail. The person will soon see where you are coming from, and so can begin a tennis match of e-mails that can rapidly become a daily source first of excitement, then furious discussion and another quickly but carefully drafted response. All this is very satisfying and, for me, what science is all about: people with nothing else in common getting very excited about their own corner of the natural world.

Last comes the real business of any collaboration. This is when tangible things like scientific materials and people start moving from one lab to another to open up experiments that would otherwise be impossible. There's little to match the excitement of receiving a parcel from abroad with potentially project-saving contents inside. And you never know, your name could end up on a joint paper!

Of course, if you have big gaps in your next paper, you need to fill them with something meaty and impressive. Collaboration is partly about using other people's expertise and equipment: visit a top lab where there's an expert who makes what you are struggling with look easy. I did this a couple of times during my Ph.D. Each time I was warmly welcomed by the people in the lab I was visiting and had a successful trip. It broadened my horizons and gave my research a real shot in the arm.

Take it from me, by going away, you can get more results, and faster, than by staying at home and putting in months of back-breaking effort trying to get a potentially nightmarish technique to work. You'll find, to your surprise, that most of your fellow scientists will happily accommodate an extra person for a week or two. Really, all you need to do is ask nicely.

One spin-off of your trip will be that you'll broaden your mind to different ways of doing the most mundane lab practices. For instance, they might do strange things with their disposable plastic-ware, and their instruments are probably unrecognisable. It really opens your mind to realise there is more than one-way to get the same result: no paths are set in stone in science, only good practice. You'll soon find yourself picking up new ideas and adding them to your ever-growing 'toolkit' of lab skills.

So, if you fancy a trip to visit another lab, just follow this simple four-point plan:

1 **Find something that you cannot do.** (Let's face it, this should not be difficult for any of us!) If you cannot find anything suitable on your long list of overdue experiments, perhaps you should think up a new one, one that might add something extra to your work. You might not be currently stuck in a rut, but I still recommend 'playing away' to have a crack at something really challenging. It'll probably impress even if you don't quite pull it off. There's nothing wrong with purposefully looking for a 'ticket' to another lab. The message: You don't have to wait until the need arises – invent the need!

2 **Establish your need to travel.** Check carefully that there are no resident experts where you currently work. You'll just have to ask around and follow-up the inevitable trail of people. I know it's a shame, but from your advisor's perspective resident experts tend to invalidate your need to travel. At least you might satisfy your boss that the only person who's tried fluorodynamic quasi-quantum spectroscopy at your place hasn't done it for years and never got it to work properly even then.

3 **Find an expert**. This will, preferably, be an expert in a prestigious lab. Let's assume you don't already have someone in mind from one of those semi-fortuitous encounters at a conference. Expand your search using the same high-flying skills you used to check for in-house experts – remember that's just talking to people and sending lots of polite e-mails! Follow my earlier guidance on e-mail etiquette.

4 **Make it happen**. Book your tickets, go to their lab and either do the experiment or learn how to do it.

To help counter too many discomforting feelings of unfamiliarity and homesickness, take a few bits of your own lab kit with you. I took this concept a little too far the first time I experimented away from home. I arrived with a massive box containing everything I might need, right down to the last pre-cut strip of laboratory film. My co-workers were possibly a little impressed, but certainly surprised, at my over-preparation.

When you arrive as a visiting worker, don't be surprised if you experience a sudden feeling of liberation. After all, you're away from the watchful eye of your boss. But don't get sloppy! You need to get as much as you can out of this trip, and it might even turn out to be a working interview. There's no better way of advertising your skills than going to work in a top lab right under the nose of your ideal boss. Even if the group leader is office-bound, word of your aptitude will soon get back to them and job offers are not unheard of! To enhance the value of your trip, make sure you go prepared to give a short presentation. This is often expected of visiting workers, even if they are only around for a week.

One last word . . . . You have to be the resourceful type to make this sort of venture work. If you arrive expecting your temporary colleagues to do all the donkeywork and just hand you the results at the end of your time there, you could be in for an uncomfortable and lonely experience.

Networking brought closer to you

Say the word 'networking' and most of us immediately think about international conferences, mobility fellowships, and other exotica, and quite right too. Away from home is where most of our connections with other scientists are initiated and then developed over time. But, there is another surprising venue for getting up close and personal with your fellow 'truth hunters' – right outside your own office door. Collaborating with other groups in your department is great, but what makes this kind of networking so worthwhile?

I once bumped into a new member of staff on my way down the corridor. I just said 'Hi' and asked how she was settling in. It turned out that my research had a lot in common with hers. Within two minutes we had discussed the work, agreed to collaborate, and even sorted out the first experiment. All without any preparation or forethought. It was, quite simply, the most 'pared to the bone' piece of networking I had ever done. Subsequently, I found myself in the middle of a flurry of less rapid, but equally useful, networking encounters right on my doorstep. Another researcher in the department who approached me prompted the second of these. He had been to one of my talks and said he had made a mental connection between one aspect of my research and his own work. Within half an hour my name was on one of his grant applications. I was stunned at the efficiency of it all. It was as if I had passed through the usual clearing process for collaborator approval (see above in this chapter) before we even started talking.

It was only at the third encounter that I started to realise what was going on. At a local workshop I met this chap from a newly opened department in a nearby institution. Our research had a bit in common even though we work on completely different systems. Within a couple of weeks we had visited each other's labs to check out the facilities. Whilst it was not appropriate for us to collaborate, it proved to be a most useful exercise as we agreed to share our resources for the common good. So *what* was going on? Sure, my efforts to get recognised within the wider scientific community could have been paying off, but there was more to it than these people simply putting a face to my name. People from across the world see my face, and countless others, at conferences all the time. Nor was it institutional pride – these people weren't networking with me merely out of a sense of loyalty or camaraderie. Then the penny dropped.

It was just easy, convenient. The advantage all of us have in our workplace is that we are surrounded by other scientists pretty much every day of the week. This means we can maintain informal relationships with each other just by popping our head around the door. We are, after all, social creatures and our brains cope much better with the idea of working with people who are around us than people who only exist in our inboxes. We get to see and hear what the others are up to in the lab and get a feel for whether there are any areas ripe for collaboration, as well as whether they are any good at what they do.

It hit me that my discovery wasn't so novel – I had just stumbled upon what more senior colleagues have been doing for most of their careers: local networking, the easiest and perhaps the most productive form of all. I felt as if I had moved on up to the next level in the game, even if I was a little slow out of the blocks. So, for any of you who have not made this connection before either, some simple rules:

1 **Think local**. Don't think of networking just as something you have to travel to do. Some of the most valuable conversations you can have are just outside your own office door.
2 **Talk to everyone**. Especially try new members of staff. They are usually dead keen to work with anyone who is already in the department as this shows they can indeed hit the ground running.
3 **Put yourself about a bit**. Visit anything that is new: new departments and buildings, new meetings and forums. There

is always a local wave to catch (often with some money floating in it), and you need to get yourself and your surfboard right in there. You might need to stretch the connection a bit between your own work and what's going on, but that doesn't seem to matter. After all, you are local and you are showing an interest, so come on in!

12

Supervising students in the lab

To some people, the journey from school to post-doc must seem like a ridiculously long one. Looking back, I realise that the only thing I ever really disliked during all those years was that 'perpetual student' tag. But eventually I gained the respect of my nearest and dearest. 'You mean, you've actually got people working for you!', my brother once exclaimed, clearly impressed. I had just mentioned one of the undergraduate project students I was supervising in the lab. It suddenly dawned on me that, yes, I now have my own people: a couple of students and a part-time technician. But, if the idea of an extra pair of hands or two is appealing, it nonetheless needs careful consideration. You need to recruit someone worthwhile – so how can you improve your chances of attracting the golden candidates from amongst the undergraduate and Masters student population? And, when you've got them, how do you make best use of their time?

During your Ph.D. you probably showed undergraduate students or fellow post-grads how to use equipment or learn a new technique, but directing what research someone else does is a different kind of challenge. As a post-doc and fully paid-up researcher, you should be in the business of collecting growing lists of possible experiments. But, with the prospect of an extra pair of hands, how do you decide what on your list is worth 'putting up' for an undergraduate or master's degree project? One option is to pick a long shot and hope for one of a long line of students to strike gold, even though it is unlikely to produce anything much in inexperienced hands. Alternatively, you may select something uninspiring but more achievable. You know, either something that should be done but is just too boring for you to get around to, or something unlikely to ever reach the top ten in your priorities.

Early in your career, you are naturally focussed on getting papers out, so why not err heavily towards achievable goals. When designing a project, I hope the student's results might provide a useful pilot for a new experiment or even a table in my next paper. Only in moments of wild abandon do I consider the prospect of a little paper all of its own.

As you probably have a list of experiments that, let's face it, would take ten years just to pilot, don't give your prospective helpers too many choices – it'll just overwhelm them. Neither should you make the project sound too rigid, as your description may not appeal to the one person who might have taken it on. Finally, make sure the techniques are fairly easy to learn, because even the most capable student is inexperienced and on a tight time limit. You want your student to be able to turn the handle and watch at least some decent results slowly emerge.

Once you've selected an offering from your list, you need to sell it. Writing project outlines is a creative art, the sole aim of which is to entice large numbers of the most capable students to plead with you to let them work for you night and day for no pay. OK, OK, more realistically you want at least a couple of people showing cautious interest when most students probably wouldn't look twice at your area of research. So, you've got to make the project sound really sexy. Have a good look at your research. Identify any areas that might provide eye-catching keywords for your project outline: you know, cutting-edge techniques or anything remotely associated with a nasty disease or explosions.

Pack your short project outline with your attractive keywords and, above all, make it sound exciting but achievable. Bear in mind that you are selling yourself as well as your project. You are competing for students, and for many their main concern will be whether the project supervisor is nice or nasty. If you haven't done much teaching yet, they clearly won't know the first thing about you. As an unknown entity, don't expect to have to reinforce your office door to withstand the rush.

Be professional and arrange to informally 'interview' any respondents. It's not surprising if you find yourself being a bit keen to get any 'early birds' on board. After all, you don't want to end up with someone who's predicted to earn a third-class degree and only had you down as his or her fifth choice. Having said this, don't make the mistake I made when my first potential candidate came knocking on my door. He was up for a 'first' and I got too excited. I bombarded him with information and ideas and showed him where everything was as if he were starting the following Monday. Bless him, he tried to show enthusiasm, but, in truth, by the end of half an hour I must have scared him senseless. With my second potential candidate (hoping for a 2:1 degree), I tried much less hard to impress. A quick tour of the lab and an even quicker demo of the type of thing they'd be doing seemed enough to prompt a flurry of questions. This enabled me to reassure them about their ability to do the work, get on with me, and write the thing up: my first lesson in student pastoral care.

Two Masters degree project students I once supervised were at opposite ends of the scientific aptitude spectrum. One was a born scientist. You know, methodical, switched on, careful with expensive equipment. The other was not quite there yet on all three counts. I'm being charitable. I had to learn fast how to find time in my own experiment-filled day to supervise someone who was a genuine help and regularly turned out useful results, along with someone who, although it wasn't their fault, was an unproductive drain on my time and energy.

Your boss is probably an old hand at dealing with project students. I know mine was. His approach was to pour attention on the 'natural scientist' type of student and leave the other to

87

flounder. But, what if some of the so-called 'no-hopers' just need a little encouragement? For instance, what if your apparently world-class slacker is paralysed deep down by a secret fear of failure? Or maybe the student who insists on ploughing a lonely, unproductive furrow is just embarrassed at the thought of asking you yet another 'stupid' question. Whoever I'm working with, I make an effort to get to know them a bit. A little genuine interest goes a long way, and, if offered early enough, might iron out issues before they become problems. I've witnessed a project student, who looked unlikely to produce anything, coming good in the end largely thanks to one kind person who noticed their predicament and, crucially, was prepared to give up quite a bit of their time to help.

If a potential winner selects your project, then you're in luck. Devote your time to them and spend some of your precious grant money while they're hands are still available. But, despite your best efforts, there will always be a few individuals whose general incompetence (breaking things), unreliability (not turning up), and/or low productivity (not comprehending the concept of a full day's work) persist. At the end of the day, it's their degree, so you'll have to resign yourself to simply moaning to your boss and putting up with them until they move on. In truth, most students will be between these two extremes: some natural aptitude but with a great need to acquire science-related skills.

It goes without saying that the few hours of effort a month it takes to keep your methods organised (and bang up-to-date) offers a massive time saving compared with tracking down your notes from scratch for each new student. In addition, writing down brief instructions specific to each project is likely to prevent at least a few minor queries later on. These should give the student some of the useful little knacks that you wouldn't dream to include in your official methods, because an adept scientist would already know them. Stuff such as exactly how to hold the instrument at the right angle, that sort of thing.

Also, regularly drawing up a list of outstanding tasks or experiments, say each week, will help your student to remember what they are supposed to be doing. Try to keep the information content down to achievable short-term targets. I know that anything more would have overwhelmed me when I first started out in this game. Lists written up with my boss certainly helped me during my loneliest moments up on the rock-face of my Ph.D. For want of a better word, a list can also form a sort of 'contract', laying down what you and your student agreed they should do. This will also help you to keep track. With my head so full of my own research, I often completely forget the experiments I suggested to my students a week ago.

Students for whom English is not necessarily easy offer an additional challenge to the fresh-faced supervisor. I once had to explain exactly how a new piece of software worked to a student with an apparently fair ability to understand English, but whose pronunciation was painfully difficult to follow. Even if I really concentrated on what they were saying, I could only be sure of two words out of every three. Writing it all down was the only way we could get anywhere. Be patient.

Drum in the need for replication. For some reason the need to overcome the vagaries of Nature by doing it again and again and again is rarely intuitive in students, myself once included I might add. Also, be sure to stress the need for accurate recording of the outcomes, even for ideas that fell flat on their face, as well as the importance of labelling which sample is which. Poor, or even worse, no labelling has an unremarkable ability to cause misinterpretation of results and the unnecessary waste of perfectly good experiments. Its incidence amongst novice scientists is endemic. I admit that I often used to think I'd simply remember what tubes A and B were!

The nature of research often makes it impossible to have set times when you can deal with queries. Dealing with unexpected interruptions with good humour is essential for happy lab life. Take it as a compliment that your advice and expertise are in

89

demand. It always makes me realise just how far I've come. Try to keep your interventions brief and give your student just enough to get right back on the scientific 'horse' if they've fallen off. But, despite all your detailed notes and many words of encouragement, the hands-on nature of science dictates that you'll often have to get, well, hands-on. I once stepped in when several attempts at verbal guidance had produced nothing. After 20 minutes we had solved the problem and, to boot, noticed a new phenomenon well worth pursuing. When it comes off, this sort of kick starting adds a real buzz to project supervision. One of your most important jobs as a post-doc is to be a problem-solver, a trouble-shooter.

Above all, remember that it's their project too, even though in some cases you might feel that you are more motivated and interested in the results than your student is. If the project's only value is that your student learns how not to do science, then your time and effort may have been worth it. If they are anything like me, it'll save them wasting time at the start of their Ph.D. making all the simple mistakes.

13

Teaching

Freed from the steep learning curve of a Ph.D. and not yet burdened by a snowdrift of administrative paperwork, post-docs are *the* full-time researchers, are they not? Yet, if you are ever to aspire to have your own independent research group, you must get hold of the teaching skills you will need when faced with the demands of your first lecturership. Teaching is also one excellent way to learn how to improve your ability to communicate science. We all know the pre-eminence of excellent communication skills amongst the most successful members of our research communities. OK, so a class of first-year under-graduates may seem a world apart from our peers at a scientific conference, and we might need to dumb down quite a lot to reach them with our message. But, in all instances, we should adapt our content and delivery to suit our audience. And, if you are able to tailor your message to make it interesting and access-ible to undergrads, then doing the same thing for your peers should be a piece of cake. It really is just a question of selectivity.

One of my first challenges on this long walk to lecturer status was self-imposed. I volunteered not only to run an undergradu-ate practical class, but also to design it from scratch. I found that the time-honoured practical class can be a microcosm of teach-ing practice. My first ideas were either only suitable for a lesson in high school or were part of my own research, rephrased and typed out to look like something they weren't: an undergradu-ate practical class! So I asked myself, 'What is an undergraduate practical meant to achieve?' Of course, students should learn something from a practical, and preferably something that will be of value to them if and when they come to face real science head on. But, a good practical class should, above all, capture their imagination and let them experience the scientific method first hand. At the end of the class, they should feel like scientists, even if the discovery was made years ago. Perhaps the key learning target, aside from any subject-specific information they pick up, should be the dawning realisation that, if your practical work is sloppy and you don't really make much of an effort, then you'll get meaningless results you can't trust. I still remember the first time I experienced the thrill as an undergraduate of knowing that my spot-on results were down to my precise and accurate work. That particular practical class certainly had quite an impact on me.

But what does all this mean, in practice, for how practical classes should be organised? Here are seven key points:

1 **Practical classes are not research**. A practical is not a piece of original research or even anything closely related. When you are so engrained in your own projects, it's hard to think outside the limits of what you are doing right now, especially as this is what you know most about. So, forget your list of successful recent experiments. Base your practical on something published, if not widely accepted.

2 **Keep it interesting**. You may find many things interesting, but keep in mind who you are talking to. Try to remember what it was about science that turned you on at that stage in your studies. One thing is sure, they'll soon lose interest if they don't see the point. Why bother to write a lesson plan at all if you don't grab their attention and stick something deep in their memory?

3 **Be visual and obvious**. It must be accessible to each person in a class possibly numbered in three figures.

4 **Make sure it works**. If you pilot your practical well, there's no reason to think it won't work on the day. But, hey, this is

Nature we're dealing with, remember, so make it robust and achievable.

5 **Make sure it is quick**. The pressure is often to reduce formal contact hours. If you are lucky, you'll have a couple of hours in which to get your message across. Remember, as in any act of information exchange, you must have a clear and simple message.

6 **Keep it fairly cheap**. Don't expect to recover any materials for reuse, as a lot of it will be trashed.

7 **Keep it reasonably safe**. There's a lot undergraduates aren't allowed to do, so check out what you can and cannot give them to handle.

Even if you follow all these guidelines, you might still be unsure how much work is enough, although I guess that too much is better than not enough. Yet, thinking back to my undergraduate days, I despised any practical class that, even if we worked flat-out and shared the tasks, we still couldn't come close to finishing in the time we had available. With this in mind, I try not to antagonise my students. I set what I think is a achievable amount of work (loafers excluded), but build in ideas for further experiments if time allows. I also add a short list of questions that can be completed during the class by the fast-finishers or tackled later by the more meticulous types. (I wonder which group you think will make the better scientists.)

Having written yourself a lesson plan to help you guess the timing, put a lot of effort into the handout – and I am deliberately using the singular here. Keep it brief and informative, and, where necessary, **SPELL IT OUT IN BOLD TYPEFACE**. Include a short introduction to get your students' heads in gear, and tell them exactly what they have in front of them and precisely what to do, step-by-step in chronological order. If none of the undergraduates can get it to work, the buck stops with you. Your idea for the practical was intended to be, quite literally, foolproof, and you'll have sold it to your boss as such. So, imagine the deep personal embarrassment you'd feel if your class were a flop, especially if you have experienced discreet grumbling among your fellow demonstrators when other people's practicals have not quite turned out according to plan.

A word of warning: there is *always* a last-minute hitch immediately before the practical. Seeing a practical class in preparation for the first time (rather than just turning up for the demonstrators' meeting) shocked me. When I was an undergraduate, I really had no idea what went into creating a practical class. I seem to remember thinking, 'This must have been done at least a hundred times before.' What I didn't realise was that, even if it was an old favourite of my lecturer, it probably hadn't been attempted since the previous year. In the intervening time, staff have come and gone, courses have changed, teaching equipment has sat unused and may (or may not) decide to work again, and the course co-coordinator has forgotten where he or she saved the master copy of last year's practical schedule.

All of this means that preparation usually starts from scratch each year. In my case, the whole practical was new and, in real terms, I was it – as far as personal knowledge and experience went. In addition to these revelations, I discovered that running practicals is rarely at the top of project leaders' agendas. A subset of results-hungry research leaders even view all undergraduate teaching as a nuisance. This can lead to a very last-minute approach – an ideal breeding ground for last-minute hitches – you know, those minor inconveniences such as the main assay not working at all. On the day before other people's practicals, I have heard the air filled with cries of: 'Hold on, check it again, it's got to work!' and 'Has anybody filled in a health and safety form for this yet?' Knowing what I know now, I am amazed that some of the practicals I've had the pleasure of demonstrating in were pulled off at all.

A TYPICAL UNDERGRADUATE TEACHING SCENARIO

It's the day of my first class and I am fighting my way through the crowds of students waiting in the corridor. My first impulse is to head in the opposite direction, but, against my better judgement, I press on and enter the teaching lab. Seeing everything neatly laid out, just as I requested, calms me down a bit. At this moment, I know I am well prepared.

Addressing and taking control of 100 students is not for the faint hearted. To get their attention, I, rather surprisingly, find myself bellowing at them as if I were some sort of ex-military type running an Outward Bound course: 'OK, let's get started then.' I don't really have a plan for taking control, but it seems to work. They all turn to listen to me. An unnervingly silent moment follows when I just look at them and they just look at me. Weird!

Before I know it, I dive straight in and start to explain the gist of what they will be doing, referring everything back to my carefully prepared practical schedule. Then comes my first true sense of relief. Once I've told them to get started, they turn away and a satisfying hubbub begins, with much shuffling and chattering. My class is up and running!

Most students are quite able to read and digest a practical schedule and follow suitably clear instructions. This is, of course, contrary to the sometimes deeply ingrained opinion held by some seasoned academics that most undergraduates are a bit dim. To be modern in our thinking, we should, of course, consider such opinions to be entirely antediluvian and the direct consequence of inadequate teaching skills – not a reflection of the students' alleged ineptitude.

Without a moment's hesitation, I saunter into the throng. Anyone who shows the slightest interest in asking a question is treated to an enthusiastic dose of encouragement. I'm really eager to see if my experiment will work in their hands. All fear and nervousness has evaporated. I'm enjoying myself.

Although one or two groups have adopted a peculiarly ham-fisted approach, which will prevent any possibility of success, most people are getting it to work and, I believe, they are learning something.

I also learn a useful lesson: be prepared to adapt to the circumstances and, if necessary, cut things out if they aren't working. Trying to be scientific, I ask the students to weigh out a reagent, although I know it would work if they just guess the amount. Seeing the queue for the digital balance, I stand up and fill the air with the cry, 'Listen up, just add about half of the "X" you've got in the tube.' At the end of the day, you want things to run smoothly and students to get the message, not to stick blindly to the schedule.

Lecturing can be equally unnerving: finding yourself in front of a class of adult faces eagerly awaiting your nugget-like revelations on the wonders of science. Follow the rules that apply for any oral presentation (see Chapter 5). The first time I lectured I had masses of material prepared, more than enough, or so I thought! I ran out of material very quickly. My first lesson in how to teach: 'time flies'. My second lesson was: 'Go slowly at first; very, very slowly.' Despite my attempts to dumb down, I later learned that hardly anyone had understood my message. Slowly the teaching becomes the easier bit – I realised this after one lecture when I didn't have a splitting headache afterwards. Students are well behaved (mostly), so little discipline is needed. I guess unlike teaching in schools you can appeal to their maturity when seeking to 'rein them in' if they get a little fidgety during a lecture. My students seem to look up to me as a researcher. It makes me realise just how much knowledge I have accumulated over my years in academia, and how much jargon has become second nature to me. It is essential that you can think from a novice's point of view and are able to express complex ideas using simple words. You also have to spot when you've 'lost them'. Watch their faces and you'll soon tell if (a) they haven't got a clue, (b) they really need a mental breather, (c) they're just plain bored by the subject matter. Needless to say, only (b) has a quick-fix solution: slacken the pace.

14

Writing grant proposals and fellowship applications

We all know that the best form of post-doc funding is a fellowship – in theory, your passport to a permanent career as a scientist. That is, if you take full advantage of the opportunity and don't experience an extended run of bad luck. But, even if you believe that you have a scientifically achievable idea that is of international importance, knowing whether *now* is the right time to apply for a fellowship often leaves post-docs in a quandary. Of course, you have to keep in mind that most fellowships have eligibility criteria, including an upper age limit or maximum number of years of post-doc experience. But, if you apply too soon, you'll probably not even be short-listed. In this context, I guess 'too soon' really means applying before you have accumulated enough high-impact publications. Let's face it, papers aren't everything, but without them all the scientific potential in the world won't get you very far.

So, if your publications list is looking a little sparse right now, why go to all that bother? Making the application could easily wipe out a couple of weeks when you could be cracking on in the lab. You may be fortunate enough to still have an alternative: bide your time; hold your nerve. Going for another post-doc grant will give you at least another year to gather more papers before that fellowship deadline looms again.

Sure, you could apply for any run-of-the mill post-doc job you see advertised in *New Scientist*. But, co-authoring another grant proposal with your current or prospective boss allows you ownership of the idea, building up a reputation as an independent thinker, which can count for a lot in your future job applications. Creating your own post-doc position (see Chapter 10) also gives you some fine control over the future direction of your career. Decide early in your current contract what to focus on for your next grant. The key here is to think fundability. Check out the priority areas and initiatives on the Web site of whichever funding body you are applying to. They may also fund ideas that do not strictly fit in, as long as they are great and achievable. So it may be a good move to pick up the phone and ask them whether they would be interested in funding your project.

Someone older and wiser than me once said that the ideal situation when writing a grant proposal is to have most of the results in hand before you apply. That way you are virtually guaranteed future success and, as a result, yet more grant income. But, how do underlings like us ever achieve this seemingly impossible goal? After all, we only have good hypotheses. Whilst other competitor applicants might have the figures already prepared for the paper when they apply for their next grant, you, almost certainly, will not. The task is no less than breaking into this exclusive club of established group leaders, who are all thinking and working three years ahead of the rest of us. There's no easy answer except to say that, whilst still keeping on top of your primary research, you somehow need to amass other, possibly unrelated, results that are (a) firm enough not to vanish into the ether at the third replicate and (b) novel enough to warrant your favourite funding body throwing a quarter of a million at it. No mean feat.

What's needed is some ruthless targeting of effort towards areas of your field that are hot but perhaps overlooked. This can feel a bit like hunting for scraps from beneath your master's table. 'How am I going to find time for yet more experiments?' I can hear you, quite rightly, say. But to make this approach worthwhile, you actually need surprisingly little by way of new results. One or two pilot experiments can give you a start. OK, so it might not be a complete set of results all ready to write up and

98

submit but at least it's better than just a good idea with no supporting evidence. But, clearly, the less speculative it seems, the more likely the project is to be funded.

Nothing focuses the mind on the 'paper-value' of your research like the pressure to earn a crust. Many scientists despise the funding pressures that force us to jump through the paper-writing hoop too early. The argument goes that the pressure to publish early leads to shortsightedness and, consequently, bitty papers. As someone who is often frustrated at how slowly science moves forward, I find this paper-mania rather useful. It forces me to focus on why I bother to do what I do, although I accept it confines us all to tackling problems that can be 'solved' inside 36 months. We all know instant results are what those who control the coffers want, so who are we to argue? The message: if you have a good idea, don't just throw it into a grant application – do the pilot experiment and get that result in hand. A picture speaks a thousand words, and may well help you to get that fellowship or grant.

PART IV

Making it in science

15

Culturing your image

Often, when you listen to a scientist being introduced before a keynote lecture, you will hear that the person started out studying something quite different from his or her current field. Also, scanning back through other people's complete publication lists (not the censored ones on scientists' own Web sites) shows just how frequently scientists change direction early on in their careers. So, for those of you who are currently slogging away in positions less than well suited to your temperament and personal abilities, take heart, you can jump ship. You needn't worry about whether or not it will be detrimental to your track record. Just be upfront and nonchalant, and make sure you talk about it in a positive light – changing scientific discipline makes you a multidisciplinary person; you are able to reinvent yourself to follow your interests. At the end of the day, you don't have to stick with what you've done just because that's what you know most about. And, in any case, your resumé is more than a list of techniques mastered – remember all those people who bang on about transferable skills? Your major selling point is your aptitude to tackle and solve new problems. Top scientists don't flap if they need to use a new instrument and have never handled the beast before, they just find someone to teach them the basics and get on with it. This slightly arrogant attitude to learning new skills is part of the pathway to success.

Your first post-doc job is an opportunity to diversify into an adaptable, well-rounded performer, who knows the score and can deliver results. So, once you have been given the springboard, not to mention the financial breathing space, of your first post-doc, set aside some brain time to find exactly what you love – and hate – about the work. Recognising what you loathe in the lab is as important as recognising what lights your fire. First take a long hard look at who you really are. If you can take a step back and then make a conscious decision to go for a specific field, you probably stand a better chance of avoiding the heartache of becoming highly employable in an area of research you just can't stomach.

So, if you are seated rather sadly in a sparkling white laboratory dreaming of the great outdoors, or are feeling miserable as you stand up to your knees in a muddy estuary and dream of wearing those sexy latex gloves that proper scientists wear, I suggest you follow your instincts. Admit that sooner or later you need to be yourself when you're at work – and that's when you'll start to enjoy it. My Ph.D. boss once told me that the Ph.D. to post-doc transition could be my last chance to reinvent myself. However, I interpreted these words of wisdom to mean that, like a budding young actor, I should avoid getting typecast in my first starring roles. My nightmare was to overhear people saying, in reference to my Ph.D. work, 'Oh, he's the one who. . .' I can't say that I did a complete makeover, but I did take charge of my career and began to shape my own scientific persona.

There are also, broadly speaking, two other ways to pigeonhole a scientist. You are either an ideas person or you are a techno-wizard. In my experience, the ideas people often look down on the techno folk with a snobbish sense of intellectual disdain. Maybe this is just a posh way of disguising jealousy. (Ideally, I guess we all want to be perceived as being quite a bit of each type). As a post-doc you want to gain respect from your new scientific peer group. First, think about how you want to be perceived. Aside from being viewed as someone with really good ideas who is technically innovative, you also need to be regarded as at least some of the following:

Reliable. You follow through and do what you say. You don't just talk; you act and act promptly. So, write that report, send that sample in the post, and follow up that offer of help you made.

Industrious. I don't think anyone would respect you for sleeping in the lab, but at least put in a full day's work. As they say, work smarter, not harder. Look at ease as you spin your many plates in the lab. If you can, avoid getting ruffled – it makes it look like you can't cope.

An individual. As long as it works and doesn't annoy anyone, do it your way. This gets you noticed. We all have to conform to a certain degree to be integrated into our institutions, but let people know you are not afraid to be yourself. As a result, people will think, quite rightly, that what you say and do is the real deal.

Composed. Never talk over your head, but be confident, as if what you do is no big deal for you. Be friendly, smile, and relax. Never appear cocky or smug. Scepticism and enthusiasm are uneasy partners, but they make a winning duo.

A champion networker. Form far-flung contacts, find suppliers and equipment all over the place, and save heaps of money by shopping around. (Bosses particularly love this.)

The list could go on, but you get the picture. Forging a successful career in science is largely about image and perception. The process of getting yourself recognised takes years, so you need to start getting your face known in the big bad world outside of your department as soon as you can. This calls for some pretty high-level networking. So far, you've probably mingled with your fellow post-grads and chatted with the odd post-doc, but talked in depth only with those project leaders you've had to. What about targeting the really scary people? You need to find the confidence to walk right up to people and start a conversation. Becoming a 'Dr' really helps with this. You are playing with the big boys now, but they really are just people. It might take a lot of guts to ask a question after their presentation, but it's a heck of a lot easier once you get them on their own. So long as you don't make yourself look like an unwanted hanger on, take any opportunity to hobnob it with these people. Conferences are the obvious choice, but you'd be amazed how many important visitors you can arrange to bump into at your own place of work. It's a no-no to talk about yourself first, so make sure you have one or two questions up your sleeve that'll interest them.

There may come a point quite early in your scientific career when you get the feeling that you might actually manage to find, and squeeze into, a permanent niche in the increasingly crowded house party that is twenty-first-century science. Despite the ongoing lack of guaranteed employment, the mostly still unpublished work, and the wish list of unfunded ideas, there can come a point when you glimpse your future mapped out before you, even through the inevitable haze cast by all that uncertainty. When this moment arrives you can see a glimpse of yourself as a credible new member of your research community: your own lab, your own funding, at least some control over your own future. As a potential future principal investigator (PI); (see Chapter 18) you need to be pushy enough to speak to lots and lots of current PIs. Ask the right questions when you do this and you will soon discover that few, if any, were ever certain that they would 'make it'. Take heart. Any doubts you are experiencing are nothing unusual.

This elusive 'credibility' factor comes largely from having something that the other members of your research community do not have. This could be the result of a discovery or invention on your part – it matters not which. The reality of this credibility reaches your conscious mind when you become aware that the PIs in your community see the advantage of having you join their club. How do they first get to see this advantage? Well, if they are in the dark about your potential benefits, and they surely are if you are a newcomer, you have to go out and tell them!

To make your mark on the world stage, you need to be an expert communicator. And, to be a successful expert communicator, you need a nice big juicy message to communicate; something that will make them sit up in their seats and take notice of you. To maximise your 'juiciness factor', you may well have to stick your neck out and talk about your results before they are accepted for publication. This is often an inevitable consequence of one form of 'early career syndrome': your struggle to get your work published before you are well known. (If you work in a famous group, you face a different form of the syndrome – showing you are your own person). But you can make these unpublished results work for you well before they reach the printed page. They are the fuel for your grant applications and for your reputation.

Getting your name 'out there' is the single most important thing you can do early in your career. Stake a claim to being a valid member of the scientific community by giving lots of presentations. But don't be so deadpan in your delivery that you give your audience the impression that you don't fully realise what your results mean. Unless they can see you are a bit of a 'player', they won't even let you into their game. So, to achieve this player status, when you present your work play it right down the line, but still make sure you don't give too much away. As the saying goes, 'Be as innocent as a lamb, and as wily as a fox.' Shrewdness is a valuable attribute in this cutthroat world of competitive science. Tell them just enough to show that you realise exactly how important your results are: important enough not to be too open about them until the acceptance letter arrives from that nice journal editor. But don't annoy people by touting yourself as some new big shot. Humility and full deference to all your collaborators will make you look even more like a successful networker. There's a surprisingly fine line between doffing your cap and appearing obnoxious. My first realisation that I must have impressed the right people came when an eminent PI approached me immediately after one of my presentations and offered to collaborate. 'Now this is more like it', I thought to myself. Like I said, I must have had something they wanted.

The way science works really is very simple when you consider its befuddling array of unspoken rules (see Chapter 10) through the right mental lens. The ability to read this hidden code may be a sign that you have what it takes to enter deeper into your community. The hidden simplicity is this: PIs want success. Success, to all intents and purposes, equates directly with high-impact publications. Unless their field's horizon is widened by new groups staking their claim and injecting new ideas, existing PIs will gradually see their own papers and citations start to dry up. Pushing forwards the boundaries of science is a community effort. So each PI is dependent on the growth, or at least maintenance, of their field to provide more data to grease the scientific wheels in their mind. The paradox is that they are simultaneously dependent upon and, at least in principle, in competition with other PIs in their field.

With time you'll speak to enough different eminent people to realise that they've been talking to each other about you, and hopefully what they are saying is complementary. A key indicator of your credibility is whether people you've never met know who you are when you first meet them. When this fateful day arrives you know that you are well on the way to success.

16

You and your big ideas

Early in your career, research can feel like a relentless round of grant and fellowship applications, posters, talks, and reports, not to mention boundary-pushing experiments. You can sometimes feel like a production-line worker in a world-class assembly plant. One of the obvious pitfalls of this time is that you can become more and more focused on your research, and lose sight of the big picture. This diminishes your chances of enriching your research by cross-fertilisation from other fields. Even at the earliest stage in your career, you really need to make these cross-links. Why? Because they could provide the ammunition you need to convince the powers-that-be that you're on to the 'next big thing' – your passport to a fellowship or an academic post.

So, how can you expand the breadth of your knowledge en route to that independent job? There are many simple ways. As far as reading goes, time demands mean that post-docs can no longer fritter away half a day in the library scouring obscure journals as they used to in their graduate student days. Abstract scanning is part of the answer, even more so if you're not in a position to access the full contents of all the weird and wonderful journals themselves. A lot of this general fishing around can be made much easier with discipline-specific Web sites such as biology's Faculty of 1000 (faculty of 1000.com). Other scientists' home pages are also good primers for an unfamiliar area. The best ones contain an overview of their research and a lot of useful information and links, including free downloads of the author's published papers. The really exciting thing about the age we live in is that everything seems to be at your fingertips. I once accessed the Web page of someone, previously unknown to me, who I immediately saw as a potential collaborator. I clicked on the e-mail button and had a new contact almost within the hour.

Regarding conferences (see Chapter 7) don't feel you have to follow the crowd. At least for part of the time, try letting your colleagues cover the mainstream sessions. Meanwhile scan the book of abstracts for anything that arouses your curiosity. Follow your nose and you'll often stumble on something that's potentially useful, or at least fascinating. A giant hall full of posters is another goldmine for budding new ideas hunters. When you go hunting in this way you're looking for connections to your own research that nobody else in your field has spotted before. Maybe another field has already stumbled on to a new way of doing things that your colleagues haven't even dreamed of. Oh sure, if it's a winner, they'll certainly be playing catch up in a year or two. Your opportunity is to access the idea first. You might have a free rein to take a new technology or a new idea, adapt it, and make yourself the expert in your own field. Thought provoking, isn't it: areas seemingly unrelated to your science might have already thrown some light on your system without you even realising it.

Once you start digging around, it won't be long before you can mention keywords your boss has never heard of. Or, better still, he or she has heard them at conferences but doesn't know exactly what they mean. You'll instantly be tagged as the lab expert, and you'll probably be hooked on the idea of fishing around for new ideas. And the further removed from your own area of research the source of new information is, the greater the potential kudos for you. The real aces at this game even step outside the boundaries of their own particular science and start working together, chemists with engineers, biologists with physicists.

Very few of us can say that we are blessed with the ability to dream up truly original ideas. Most of us have to settle for ones that are really extensions or adaptations of what other people have already done. But the potential for attention grabbing is not diminished by that fact. So, if you fancy yourself as a bit of a maverick, start worrying a bit less about keeping up with every detail of the literature in your own field and try an exploration of foreign fields. It'll mark you out as someone who's into BIG science and it could pay rich dividends for your future career prospects. Because so few people rise to the challenge of keeping a finger on the big picture, a little bit of investigation outside your own field does go a very long way.

When you see or hear about something exciting – an unpublished result that backs up what you've long thought to be true, for example, or especially when you think up something exciting yourself – your first instinct is to tell someone else. After all, not only does it show how acute your scientific intuition is, but, if the information comes from another scientist, it also demonstrates how successfully you're developing your network of contacts. But whether you want to share your idea to impress people or to verify that it means what you think it means, BEWARE! Yes, as a trainee scientist you need to learn what is and is not worth getting excited about by checking what you've seen or heard with others. However, there comes a point, quite early in your career, when you have to learn to bite your lip and start breaking this habit of blabbering too much. It's about developing enough self-confidence to make it as an independent scientist or, to put it another way, developing trust in your own ability to reason.

Part of becoming a successful scientist is building up your own portfolio of ideas: experiments you'd love to do if you ever had the time (and money). And, if you're facing the post-doc bottleneck, the more irons you can get in your research fire the better. So allow yourself the luxury of keeping some selected information secret. Then, one rainy Friday afternoon, you can play around with an idea and see if it's worth following up. This is what successful scientists do. They get ideas (often not entirely their own), play around with them through the wonderful medium that is the pilot experiment, and then follow up the worthwhile stuff. The weak link in the chain is keeping quiet about the information in your head, possibly for years. If you ask yourself honestly, you will probably have at least some instinct to keep useful nuggets of information to yourself, or between your close and trusted confidantes. In practice, not speaking about these nuggets may prove much harder than the act of deciding not to. This is especially true if you're a motor mouth like me. OK, so it's unlikely that anyone in the bar will want to beat you to it when you tell them about the killer experiment that you think might turn your field on its head. However, you do need to curb your natural enthusiasm for sharing information when it comes to potential rivals.

I'm talking about consciously not mentioning sensitive information – for instance, e-mails to that mate of yours who works in a lab that collaborates with your main competitors. I'm talking about not disclosing everything you know at the conference poster session and not gushing information during question time at the end of your presentation. I mean learning to play it a little cagey. No, not sneaky or dishonest: I would never advocate lying to deliberately throw someone off the scent. But you can certainly accelerate your career by opting not to share all of your precious information with others.

'Hold on a minute', I hear you ask, 'What about your own boss? Isn't it naughty to keep things from him or her?' You are supposed to tell your advisor everything, right? OK, let's say you're soon to move to another lab. That hopefully close relationship you've developed with your boss is unlikely to last forever. Of course you'll stay in touch, but from now on you must consider what not to tell. This is especially true if you are moving to another group working in the same field. The vast majority of group leaders are motivated primarily by one thought – prestige. And, as we all know, prestige in the eyes of one's peers derives largely from publications. Your boss is hungry for prestigious publications. Your results and good ideas and your contacts' information are excellent food to help satisfy this hunger.

Once you've moved on, your old boss will still present your work as their own – but at least your contribution should be acknowledged. However, if you leave sensitive information and good ideas behind when you depart, expect them to be snapped up and used without a moment's hesitation. What you must realise is that by talking about your ideas, you are denying yourself an unhindered opportunity to follow them up yourself. Some people might even misinterpret your openness as disinterest in pursuing these ideas – a sort of invitation to others to experiment. I'm afraid this may be just as true of your own boss as it is of any other scientist. Sometimes you might be able to second-guess that your boss won't have the time to follow up a particular lead. In such cases it might be worth disclosing what's on your mind with the explicit intention of getting a right of first refusal. Personally, I feel much happier with this kind of arrangement. As I said, I'm a naturally open person not much good at holding secrets long term.

Choosing whether to discuss what you know with others is a key step in your push for early independence in your research career. Distasteful as it may seem, unless you learn to be selective when communicating with your peers, you may find yourself left behind in the relentless hunt for success.

17

Planning for a permanent job

Planning your independent research

Exactly what research would you be doing right now if you were given a free rein and your own independent group? Have you ever really thought about it? You may think the prospect just too far-fetched to waste time considering. I did too. But this was before I decided, amidst all the frantic hustle and bustle of everyday research life, to apply for a proper job, a permanent one. With hindsight my first shot at the big time came a bit early for me, having only just finished the post-graduate long-service award (or Ph.D. for the uninitiated). Needless to say I didn't get the job. What I did achieve was a thorough understanding of my research desires.

You see, when applying for a permanent job, a lectureship for example, a ten-year plan is what you need. Your prospective employer needs to see whether you can think big, but also whether your big plans fit in with their grand plans for the School, Institute or Department. However, a whole decade is a whopping great amount of research. We young scientists working deep in the mines of human knowledge are often so focused on the urgency of the next paper or grant application that our minds cannot deal with such hypothetical long-term scenarios. In just this overwhelmed frame of mine, I decided it was high time I took a long walk in the open air: time to reflect. I needed some space to let my mind filter out all the debris of urgent day-to-day stuff to find the kernels of insight that I needed.

At first, it was most disconcerting to realise just how small-minded I had been. For all my successes, I'd never been able to free my mind enough to think beyond the next year or two. But, after walking for two or three miles, and, after several false starts, a stream of consciousness started to flow, nebulous at first, then more precise. Remarkably, inside my mind *was* a big picture, a long-term plan of where I saw my research going. I set off for home and turned on my PC immediately: my ten-year research plan was about to be written.

I reckoned a good way to start was by writing down some background information for the non-specialists. This was easy, just like writing the first paragraph of an introduction. I deliberately used words that made it all sound terribly exciting. Next out of my brain came the other easy stuff: a list of my publications, the papers I had submitted or had under way, a list of my current collaborations, that kind of stuff. In other words, what I had achieved so far and who had already accepted me.

I was now ready to tackle the core of my plan. It's hard to just dream up a research project without giving some careful thought to where the money is. If you want to stand your best chance of securing yourself some cash, you have to convince the funding bodies that your big idea fits neatly into one of their initiatives. So I read all the spiel on the relevant Web sites and looked at what proposals had already been funded. After checking my aims against what the main funding bodies were currently going for, I felt confident my plan was highly fundable.

I then jotted down my research goals and was quite shocked when I took a second glance at them – they sounded really ambitious and cutting-edge. You know, I still can't believe I'm right in the thick of this fast-moving science game. Science is a very exciting way to earn your living. You have to learn to swim in the deep end because there is only a deep end: you are the expert. I set out to break my research plan into more manageable chunks – my short-term and long-term objectives. Naturally it was easier to include a lot more detail for my short-term objectives than for my long-term pie-in-the-sky ones. Short-term objectives are what you could, in theory, write grant proposals about right now, so they have to be really precise statements linked to real experiments. The long-term objectives are there to inspire and provide the reason why you're proposing to spend all this money.

Finally, the moment came when I had to put into words that stream of consciousness I had experienced earlier. Having pinned down the detail, I had a clear view of where I wanted to get to, but I now had to suggest how to get there. Strategies are not about specific experiments but about tools and approaches. As such they are a good place to bring up all the suitable buzzwords. A fictitious example might be: 'To achieve a better understanding of the wobble constant using a combination of spectral fuzziness telemetry and second-sight kinetics.' No specific experiments, but still saying in general terms how you intend to reach your goals.

By now I had all the elements in hand to write an actual proposal for my ten-year plan; all I had to do was put them in the right order: introduction, research goals, research strategy, long-term then short-term research objectives, potential funding sources, potential grant proposals, my publications and collaborations. I deliberately set out my potential grant proposals and funding sources together in a separate funding-strategy section. This repeated much of what was written in the research objectives, but made it clear to my prospective employer that I intended to do something about them, i.e., to write and submit grant proposals as soon as I got the job.

At the time, writing this plan was one of the most enjoyable experiences of my academic career. It still makes happy reading (at least for me) and I shall refer to it many times in the future,

I'm sure. It also made me realise that getting funded is all about finding the critical balance between researching close to the knife-edge and convincing others that you have the ability and tools to make it happen.

Preparing for the interview

For many of us the first time we face the scrutiny of a 'serious' interview panel is when we try to convince an institution to take us on as a Ph.D. student. Even if you have run the interview gauntlet before, the stakes this time – a career in science, or not – have probably never been so high. And, as you progress, applying for post-doc jobs, fellowships, and permanent academic positions, the pressure just keeps piling on.

In an interview you may have as little as half an hour to give a stunning, or at least solid, answer to the one main question from each panel member. There could easily be six or more of them, and not surprisingly the number of people gazing at you from across the table seems to increase the higher the profile of the job. At the other extreme, you could be in for a two-hour grilling session when the challenge is to stay alert and sharp, right until the end. But, whatever the format or duration of your ordeal, you need to develop a strategy that ensures you come up with the goods on the day.

In spite of the obvious need to prepare, some people still just turn up for interviews and give the first answers that come into their heads. Needless to say this usually has disastrous consequences for their chances of getting the job. Worse still, others have a well thought out strategy that vanishes as soon as the door to the interview room opens. Interviews do that to people.

In many ways an interview is like an oral examination. So why not prepare as you would for an exam? You don't know the questions beforehand, but you can revise and try to second-guess what might be asked. But, most importantly, make sure you give the right performance to get the maximum marks – all the revision in the world counts for nothing if you lose your self-control under the spotlight. As with oral presentations (see Chapter 5) the knack to a successful interview is to practice being both relaxed *and* alert. Practice is particularly essential if you feel these two states of mind are mutually exclusive.

Remember, your interviewers are testing:

1 **Can you do the job well**? How can you expect the interview panel to pin down your good qualities if you're not sure of them yourself? So get the facts about yourself clear in your mind. You may know you are strong in the lab but weak on writing up. Or you may be an excellent lecturer but poor on project management. However your SWOT (strengths, weaknesses, opportunities, threats) analysis shapes up, make sure you've sussed yourself out thoroughly and honestly before you start. Getting constructive criticism from colleagues will undoubtedly help a lot. Turn your not-so-positive attributes into something more flattering (for example, you may have to admit to being a bit messy in the lab, but sell it for what it is: your passion for success drives you to often work like crazy on five experiments at once) or demonstrate that your weaknesses are outweighed by your skills in other areas.

2 **Do they like the look of you**? It's true to say it's called an 'interview' because they call you 'in to view' you. Of course this has more to do with your attitude than with the colour of your tie or the cut of your blouse: you could seriously harm your chances with something as trivial as not smiling at all during the interview. This will be interpreted as either that you are not able to cope under pressure or that you were born miserable. Not good. You are a happy person and you are not under pressure. You are relaxed, confident. You are likely to get lots of other offers. You are on your way to the top. This is the impression you want to create. This is the head-job you need to set in concrete in your mind before you walk through that door.

3 **Do you show any strong contra-indications for either (a) or (b)?** Just one 'no-no' can turn the panel against you, even if they quite like you in all other respects. Competition is usually strong.

In a nutshell, during the whole of the interview never cease to be ENTHUSIASTIC (you're relaxed, so smile a little), ATTENTIVE (you are alert, maintaining good eye-contact and nodding a fair bit), and POSITIVE (give forward-looking answers). WARNING! Do not go to the other extreme and appear cocky. No one likes a cocky person. Even if your resumé is strong and you've come across well during the interview, a little humbleness is always a very positive thing. Expressing a willingness to learn more or admitting a small weakness will make you appear honest. It will also create the impression that 'what you see is what you get'. They'll believe everything else you've said is fair comment and probably true.

By the way, are you going for a financial services job? No! So don't dress like it. Yes, wear smart clothes, but leave the power suit in the wardrobe. You'll look and feel overdressed if you turn up looking like a young executive in a big multinational. This is science remember.

My last piece of advice would be to *never* let your guard down. Your sociability will almost certainly be tested over lunch. They'll ask people who met you on the tour of the institution what they thought of you after you've left. Everyone you encounter needs to be impressed, from the porter to the head of department. So be prepared to think on your feet and charm them all. You'll end up feeling exhausted, but, if you get your head straight before you start, you'll find it much easier to sell yourself.

18

Do you have principal investigator (PI) potential?

It has been suggested, on more than one occasion, that any reasonably intelligent, hard-working person can make it as a scientist. This statement is not to belittle scientists' mental abilities, but merely underpins the basic premise that published scientific work should be reproducible by any competent, suitably informed person. ('Suitably informed' means that you'd need to spend the best part of a decade getting academically tooled up for life as a scientist.)

Now this is all very well, but it seems to me that not everyone who could make it as a scientist can actually make it as a PI. Indeed, many research careers are deliberately shortened after the dawning realisation that there is often poor, if any, career structure for post-docs, not to mention mounting exasperation at the post-post-doc bottleneck in the permanent scientific jobs market. So who succeeds in this ruthless battle for the top of the heap? The following points are ten skills and attributes we all need if we are to make it as a PI. Before you convince yourself you are already on track for the top, you might want to ask yourself honestly if you've got what it takes.

1 **Getting your face known**. Are you prepared to plough a lot of effort into getting your face known? This will require that you are able to stomach the thought of being away from home rather a lot. First, you must get yourself recognised, and then known, by all the big names in your field, and this involves attending all the right conferences and travelling the world as

a visiting speaker to get your message out. Of course, your message in the PI market isn't your science per se, but that YOU can produce stuff of such international calibre. Naturally, if you focus too much on networking early in your career, you're going to be away from the lab for too long at the stage when there really isn't anyone to replace you. This will translate into too few publications. So, it's a fine balancing act.

2 **Papers, papers, papers**. Can you make a name for yourself as the first author on lots of big papers? Getting down to writing is hard, even harder than getting down to the umpteenth control experiment, especially when, as made clear in point 1, there's often no one else to keep turning the handle in the lab. Finding the time is all about making the time, and this usually means your own 'spare' time. But be aware that getting papers out is never a bad thing, *unless* all your publications are in journals that no one has ever heard of. Also be careful not to end up being viewed as someone else's flunky, a technical wizard with no mind of your own – that is, spending too long as first author in a group where someone else gets all the glory as the prestigious final authorship. If you can experiment or write even though you are hot, tired, and maybe sick of working like a dog, and still do it well, then maybe you've got what it takes to go all the way in this crazy, wonderful game called research. Do you get excited at the prospect of getting published? I don't know, call it ownership: you had the idea, you co-wrote the grant proposal, you did the work, and now you've virtually sweated the paper out. You should want to get your reward.

3 **Your mind**. Do you love to think about your science? Do you lie awake at night chewing it all over? Can your brain take it when others fall asleep, get bored or become impatient? Can you solve intractable problems, ignoring petty distractions to focus in hard? Faced with a blank sheet or mind-boggling complexity can you look at things in a fresh way and come up with lots of novel ideas? Can you write a good easy-to-read

review to bring it all together? Do colleagues who need some-one just to bounce ideas off consult you as a trouble-shooter? Overall, are you seen as having a good mind? If you've answered YES to most of these questions, then consider your-self adequately equipped in the mental faculties department.

4 **Ruthlessness**. Are you ruthless, constantly reappraising your research to instinctively weed out blind alleys almost before they've appeared? This question is about the ability to apply logic and probability to your wish list of experiments and the even greater ability to stick to the result, come what may. It's crucial to be able to override your natural desire to hold on to pet hypotheses or experimental approaches in which you have invested heavily.

5 **Instinct**. Do you have a sixth sense for which way your re-search should go, even when you can't give a reason why? Can you make the right decision, call it a gut feeling if you wish, when faced with a difficult choice? Instinct and inspir-ation often play unsung roles in science. I think they're grossly underrated.

6 **The knowledge**. Can you stay right on top of the literature and read extensively outside your own field, putting yourself in a position where you can recognise how recent advances in other people's fields raise opportunities in yours? Are you a nugget hunter par excellence? Do you have the ability to speed-read through the constant stream of electronic tables of contents arriving in your inbox, picking out keywords as you rapidly scroll down?

7 **Communication**. Do you have the 'gift of the gab'? Can you address packed conference halls, and grab the attention of a 100 or more students in a lecture theatre? Can you talk your way around your areas of weakness and convince people of your worth? Someone once told me the most successful scientists aren't necessarily the best scientists, they're the ones who sell (for 'sell' read 'present') their science the most convincingly.

8 **People skills**. Are you a teacher? Do you have the patience to tutor students who seem unable to grasp a word of what you've said? Can you mentor and guide young people? Are you a good manager? Even if your work doesn't involve contact with undergraduates, you'll always have more inexperienced people under you as you begin to climb the science ladder and your group grows in size.

9 **The politics**. Can you handle the politics? Science is all about personalities, sometimes personalities that are egotistical and difficult. Do you have a feel for how and when to approach people in positions of influence and power with your requests? Diplomacy and confidence are the name of the game.

10 **The real you**. Can you walk away from your work and still be human? What point is there in being a resounding success as a PI if your friends and family don't know you anymore, or if you become aloof or bigoted? This point is the biggest challenge of all if you aspire to reach the very top of the scientific tree. In my experience, there are only two types of top PIs. The very nice and the very not so nice. Which type would you be if you got to the top?

If you can answer 'yes' to all of these questions, then you may be well on your way to becoming a huge smash in your field. If not, don't worry. There are plenty of PIs and potential PIs out there with deficiencies in more than one of these areas, myself included. The trick is to recognise your weaknesses early on in your career and either work on them or work around them.

But, if you can show extreme perseverance in the face of adversity, when your experiments fail, when you lose weeks of work and have to start it all over again, when you are simply tired beyond belief; if you can overcome all this and carry on, you must be a pretty tenacious survivor. I wish you all success.

Epilogue

Few professions offer the universal mystique that surrounds being a scientist. If you can make the grade in this game, you're right up there with the secret agents. The mystical transformation from non-scientist to scientist is through the rite of passage that is the Ph.D. And, yet, this two-pronged voyage of discovery and self-discovery is just the beginning of the transformation. Life in the busy years that follow becomes more complex and demanding than you could ever have imagined. Yet, despite the frantic activity, the boredom and the frustration, you can go to parties safe in the knowledge that, if anyone asks you what you do for a living, you can answer without apologising or shrugging your shoulders: you are a scientist. Enjoy it. You are paid to play.

Web-links

Adobe Acrobat® – adobe.com/products/acrobat/main.html.

Endnote® – endnote.com

Faculty of 1000 – faculty of 1000.com

Microsoft PowerPoint® – office.microsoft.com

Speed Reading Advice – ucc.vt.edu/stdysk/suggest.html

Web of Science – wos.mimas.ac.uk

Science's Next Wave – nextwave.sciencemag.org

Index